To:

....

From:

....

Date:

....

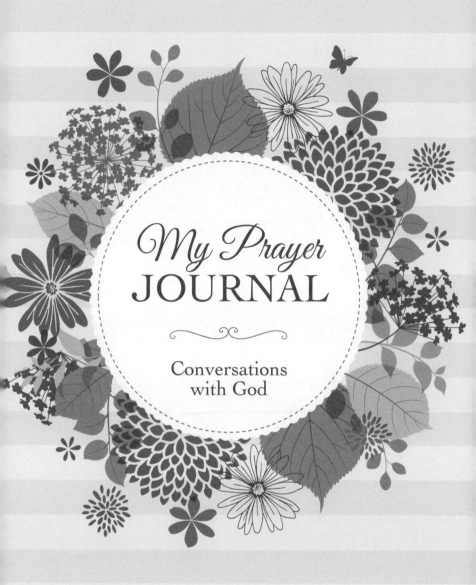

My Prayer
JOURNAL

Conversations
with God

BARBOUR BOOKS
An Imprint of Barbour Publishing, Inc.

Member of the
Evangelical Christian
Publishers Association

Printed in China.

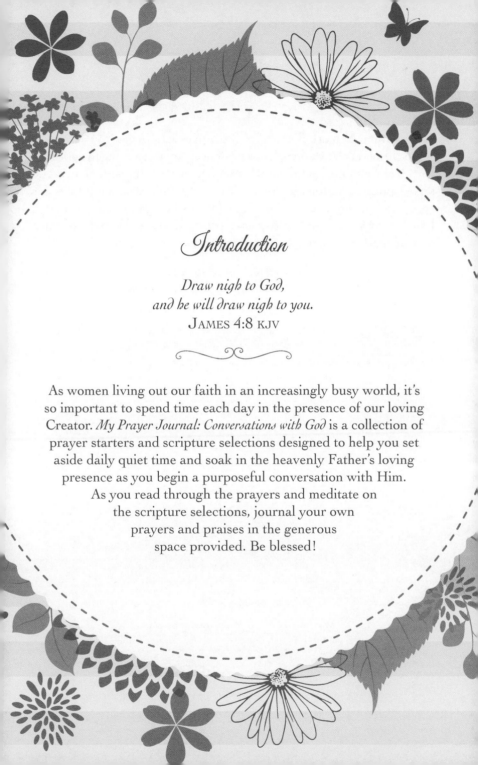

Introduction

Draw nigh to God,
and he will draw nigh to you.
JAMES 4:8 KJV

As women living out our faith in an increasingly busy world, it's so important to spend time each day in the presence of our loving Creator. *My Prayer Journal: Conversations with God* is a collection of prayer starters and scripture selections designed to help you set aside daily quiet time and soak in the heavenly Father's loving presence as you begin a purposeful conversation with Him. As you read through the prayers and meditate on the scripture selections, journal your own prayers and praises in the generous space provided. Be blessed!

Come Closer, Beloved

Dear Father, You are the God of the universe, and yet You ask me to come closer. I can't stand in Your presence, yet You ask me to approach with freedom and confidence. It's all because of Jesus, that I can do this! I praise You for the great gift of Your Son, who allows me this access to You, my Creator. I am so small, but I long to know You better. I am so weak, but I know You have power to spare. Help me to come to You again and again. In Jesus' precious name, amen.

*In him and through faith in him we
may approach God with freedom and confidence.*
EPHESIANS 3:12 NIV

....
....
....
....
....
....
....
....
....
....
....
....
....
....
....
....
....
....

The One Who Is

Heavenly Father, today I'm grateful for all You are—the God who is, the God of the living, the great I Am. Your character is unchanging. You are the epitome of perfect holiness and love. Because of who and all You are, I believe and trust in You. Your truthfulness is indisputable and Your power is established. Not just for the majestic works by Your hand but for the pure glory of Your nature—I worship You today. Amen.

Who is like the LORD our God, who dwells on high?
PSALM 113:5 NKJV

....
....
....
....
....
....
....
....
....
....
....
....
....
....
....
....
....
....

In the Inner Room

Dear God, You know how often I pray and how often I *don't*. You know that sometimes I use it as a weapon. "Lord, give me patience!" I say in the presence of those who are vexing me. Please forgive me. That is not prayer. And Lord, forgive me for *not* praying. Forgive me for wasting the quiet moments that You give me with things that will be forgotten in eternity. I want to know You now, *here*, even before I am with You forever. Amen.

> *"But you, when you pray, go into your inner room, close*
> *your door and pray to your Father who is in secret, and your*
> *Father who sees what is done in secret will reward you."*
> MATTHEW 6:6 NASB

....
....
....
....
....
....
....
....
....
....
....
....
....
....
....
....
....

I Will Hear

Dear Lord, I praise You that You are the God who hears. I praise You that You know my heart even before *I* do. I rest in the fact that You are answering my prayer, even before I pray. Help me to be more like You, Lord. So often I don't take the time to listen with love to the people around me. And while they are still speaking, I say *no*. I need Your ears and Your heart, Lord. Speak to me and through me. Amen.

"Before they call I will answer;
while they are still speaking I will hear."
ISAIAH 65:24 NIV

....
....
....
....
....
....
....
....
....
....
....
....
....
....
....
....
....
....

With This Ring

Dear Lord, You are faithful yesterday, today, and tomorrow. I thank You for giving me a husband who exemplifies that enduring faithfulness. Thank You for how he has kept the promises he made to me on our wedding day: promises to love, cherish, protect, and provide. Thank You for his hands that hold my heart so gently; thank You that he is more like Jesus than anyone I have ever known. I praise You for the great gift that he is to me. Thank You for his example of faithful love, and I pray that I would give him only joy, submission, and devotion in return. Amen.

For no matter how many promises God
has made, they are "Yes" in Christ.
2 CORINTHIANS 1:20 NIV

....
....
....
....
....
....
....
....
....
....
....
....
....
....
....
....

The Time of Singing

Father, the earth is brown and dead now, as hard as iron and as cold as stone. But I know that life lurks, waits: seeds that will spring to green life with the warming sun and a gentle rain, nests that will hold eggs the color of sky, ponds that will sparkle and sing with dragonflies and frogs. Thank You for spring, for the promise of green and new life. And thank You for heaven, where that fleeting green will never fade and fall away. Amen.

For lo, the winter is past, the rain is over and gone.
The flowers appear on the earth; the time of singing has come.
Song of Solomon 2:11–12 nkjv

....
....
....
....
....
....
....
....
....
....
....
....
....
....
....
....
....
....

The Day of Small Things

Dear Lord, I ask for thankfulness in the small things. I yearn to see each day as a gift—swathed in sunrise—to be unwrapped. Thank You, Lord, for what You gave me today: for a curl of green leaf unfurling on the winter end of a branch, for a cherry blossom like a snag of fuchsia silk, for scratchy frog songs. Thank You for moments that remind me that ordinary days are really shot through with holiness. I thank You now, Lord, for those gifts and the gifts that I will see *You've already given me* as I learn to live in thankfulness. Amen.

For who hath despised the day of small things? For they shall rejoice.
ZECHARIAH 4:10 KJV

....
....
....
....
....
....
....
....
....
....
....
....
....
....
....
....
....
....

Satisfied

Even in the midst of life's droughts—when everything seems dry and dead and dusty—thank You, Father, that You continue to water my heart and satisfy my soul. When I see others are in the midst of drought, give me the right words and actions to share Your living water that will keep them from ever being thirsty again.

And the LORD shall guide thee continually, and satisfy thy soul in drought, and make fat thy bones: and thou shalt be like a watered garden, and like a spring of water, whose waters fail not.
ISAIAH 58:11 KJV

....
....
....
....
....
....
....
....
....
....
....
....
....
....
....
....
....
....

Faithful

God, I confess to You that I have sinned. I have gone astray, away from Your love. Again and again I fall short. It shames me to admit it, but You ask for my confession. Forgive me. Wash me. Bring me home. Thank You that even now, I can rely on Your faithful love. Thank You for the promise that You are faithful to forgive me—not just yesterday and today, but tomorrow as well.

If we confess our sins, he is faithful and just to forgive us our sins,
and to cleanse us from all unrighteousness.
1 JOHN 1:9 KJV

....
....
....
....
....
....
....
....
....
....
....
....
....
....
....
....
....

The Rescue

Dear Father, tonight I watched a movie in which a sweet but foolish girl was kidnapped and sold into slavery in a foreign country. No one would help her, except her father, who crashed through every barrier and mowed down every bad guy who stood in his way. Though stabbed, beaten, and broken, he found her and rescued her and brought her home. I just started weeping, Father, when I realized that *this* is exactly what You have done for me. I was lost and alone and sold into slavery in this sin-stricken world. You *came*. You rescued me. Thank You, again and again. Amen.

"He rescues and he saves; he performs signs and wonders in the heavens and on the earth."
DANIEL 6:27 NIV

....
....
....
....
....
....
....
....
....
....
....
....
....
....
....

Blessings Instead of Curses

My Lord, I feel misused. I feel cursed. I feel slighted and abused. I'm angry and hurt. I come to You with these feelings, and I give them to You. Take away the hurt and my desire for revenge. Give me Your heart when it comes to others. I pray that You would bless the people who have made me feel this way. Your will be done, Father.

Bless them that curse you, and pray for them which despitefully use you.
LUKE 6:28 KJV

....

....

....

....

....

....

....

....

....

....

....

....

....

....

....

....

....

....

The Other Cheek

Really, God? If someone hurts me, do I really have to ask him to hurt me again somewhere else? That seems like You're asking too much! It goes against everything society teaches me about standing up for myself, about being assertive, about not being a doormat. Teach me what Jesus meant when He said this. Give me a heart that wants to follow His example. . .even when I don't want to.

Whosoever shall smite thee on thy right cheek, turn to him the other also.
MATTHEW 5:39 KJV

....
....
....
....
....
....
....
....
....
....
....
....
....
....
....
....
....
....
....

Spiritual Guardrails

Dear God, help me erect proper boundaries in my life. I don't want to fall prey to a sin simply because I wasn't being careful. Just like guardrails on a dangerous mountain highway, boundaries in my life keep me closer to center and further away from the cliffs. I know Satan is plotting my destruction, but Your power is greater. Let me cooperate with Your grace through a careful lifestyle and a discerning spirit. In Christ's name, amen.

Stay alert! Watch out for your great enemy, the devil. He prowls around like a roaring lion, looking for someone to devour.
1 PETER 5:8 NLT

Wide Awake

You know how tired I am, God. You know how weary I am of facing troubles and challenges. Help me not surrender to my exhaustion. Send godly friends into my life that can encourage me to continue on the path that You have laid for Your children. Keep me wide awake and alert, focused always on You.

Therefore let us not sleep, as do others; but let us watch and be sober.
1 THESSALONIANS 5:6 KJV

....
....
....
....
....
....
....
....
....
....
....
....
....
....
....
....
....
....
....

Cry in the Night

Dear Lord, there is never a time I cry out to You and You are not instantly listening. Unlike the false god of the prophets of Baal, You are never busy, traveling, sleeping, or too deep in thought to hear me. The only thing that stops my prayers from reaching You is my own unconfessed sin. Help me examine my heart when I fear that You are silent, and forgive my sins. I long to stand before You, complete and unashamed. Just as I run to my baby when he cries, I know I am never alone. Amen.

"Then you call on the name of your god, and I will call on the name of the LORD. The god who answers by fire—he is God."
1 KINGS 18:24 NIV

....
....
....
....
....
....
....
....
....
....
....
....
....
....
....
....

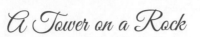

A Tower on a Rock

You, O Lord, are my place of absolute safety: a high tower built on a rock that will never move. When trials and temptations surround me, teach me to lift my gaze higher. Help me look above all my troubles and see Your tall tower—and then run there as fast as I can!

The God of my rock; in him will I trust: he is my shield,
and the horn of my salvation, my high tower, and my refuge,
my saviour; thou savest me from violence.
2 SAMUEL 22:3 KJV

....
....
....
....
....
....
....
....
....
....
....
....
....
....
....
....
....
....

The Well of Words

Lord, You've given me a love of words, and by Your grace, You've allowed me to use it. Sometimes, though, I worry that I'll run out of things to say. What if the well runs dry? But then I remember how You created everything out of nothing. You spoke, and it came to be. You are the author of life, the Word made flesh. Thank You for breathing that same spark of creativity into us along with the breath of life. I know that if I keep my eyes fixed on You, I'll never run out of words. There is no end to the ways I can praise You! Amen.

"Whoever drinks the water I give them will never thirst. Indeed, the water I give them will become in them a spring of water welling up to eternal life."
JOHN 4:14 NIV

....
....
....
....
....
....
....
....
....
....
....
....
....
....
....
....
....

Moving and Making Friends

God, I don't like change or new places. I'd rather just stay in my comfort zone. But that's not happening. Here I am in a strange new environment. I miss my old friends so much. I feel like crying just thinking about them. But that won't do any good, will it? I need some heavenly moxie. It's time to square my shoulders, walk in, smile, introduce myself, and meet some new people. I guess I can think of them as prefriends. Help me not to chicken out! Thank You. Amen.

A man who has friends must himself be friendly.
PROVERBS 18:24 NKJV

....
....
....
....
....
....
....
....
....
....
....
....
....
....
....
....
....

Mentoring

Dear God, the Bible tells older women to mentor younger women. That's an element missing from my life. Although my mom did a great job of passing along the life lessons she'd learned, and we have a good relationship, I still need the insight and affirmation of an older woman. Lord, I need a trusted confidante, one who will help me succeed. I ask You to send someone like that my way in fulfillment of Your Word. And let me fill that role myself someday when I have the required résumé. Amen.

May [the aged women] teach the young women to be sober,
to love their husbands, to love their children.
TITUS 2:4 KJV

....
....
....
....
....
....
....
....
....
....
....
....
....
....
....
....
....

The Pebble

Sometimes I feel like I have no influence, Lord. That nothing I think or do resonates much beyond the walls of this house. But You comfort and empower me with Your Word again. Thank You for reminding me that no matter what small circles we move in, we are all leaders to someone: a child, a wife, a younger brother, a boy flipping burgers in a fast-food joint, a shy new believer in church. I am a tiny pebble thrown into the sea, Lord, but my ripples will travel. Amen.

"You did not choose me, but I chose you and appointed you so that you might go and bear fruit—fruit that will last."
JOHN 15:16 NIV

Fadeless Beauty

Dear God, I'm getting older. That's not news to You, I know. You've seen my journey from day one. But now my body is revolting, and my hormones are rebelling. I don't like looking in the mirror because it shocks me to see lines on my face. Inside I don't feel old, but my body doesn't agree. Still, Lord, help me remember that my identity in You is changeless, and my beauty in You is fadeless. The magazines may say differently, but I know that in Your sight, I have a loveliness that time can't touch. Amen.

The unfading beauty of a gentle and quiet spirit, which is so precious to God.
1 PETER 3:4 NLT

Golden Words Needed

Heavenly Father, today I need affirming words. You know that words are important to me as a woman. You also know that I struggle with self-worth. The other people in my world don't always meet my need to be affirmed verbally, and I can't expect them to fill every void in my life. So, Lord, let me look to and in Your Word to find the love and encouragement I need. In Jesus' name, amen.

A word fitly spoken is like apples of gold in settings of silver.
PROVERBS 25:11 NKJV

....
....
....
....
....
....
....
....
....
....
....
....
....
....
....
....
....
....

Power

Sometimes I say, "The only thing I can do now is pray." I mean that I've done everything I could think to do, and now as a last resort, I'll fall back on prayer. Forgive me, Father, for trusting in things that are not from You and for setting my mind on worldly things. Remind me that prayer is never the last resort and that You are faithful in hearing it. Teach me to see the power that prayer can unleash in the world.

The effectual fervent prayer of a righteous man availeth much.
JAMES 5:16 KJV

....
....
....
....
....
....
....
....
....
....
....
....
....
....
....
....
....
....

Divine Guidance

Dear Lord, it's so hard sometimes to know what Your will is. You don't write specific instructions in the sky nor emblazon them on a marquee. So how can I know exactly what You want me to do? How can I keep from making a big mistake? How can I proceed with this decision? I ask today that You would give me wisdom; send me guidance as I seek Your will. Through a person, a thought, a scripture, let me sense Your leading for this situation. I want my life to honor Your plan for me. In Christ's name, amen.

If any of you lacks wisdom, you should ask God, who gives generously to all without finding fault, and it will be given to you.
JAMES 1:5 NIV

....
....
....
....
....
....
....
....
....
....
....
....
....
....
....
....
....

In Your Presence This Day

Dear Father, I thank You that Your ear is always listening for the cries of Your people. You are always listening for my voice, and You know it out of billions of others. My words are not just spoken to the empty air, but You give them Your attention. Forgive me for my sins today, Lord, for they are many. I rest under Your mercy.

"If my people, who are called by my name, will humble themselves and pray and seek my face and turn from their wicked ways, then I will hear from heaven."
2 CHRONICLES 7:14 NIV

....
....
....
....
....
....
....
....
....
....
....
....
....
....
....
....
....

Everything Is Possible

How amazing, Lord—my Father is the Creator of the universe! Your infinite creativity formed the beauty of the earth and the intricacies of life. I know I can rest assured in Your strength, in Your might, in Your abilities. There's nothing on heaven or on earth that You can't handle. Forgive me when I try to take things into my own hands. Since You made the world and everything in it, I know You can take care of my small life!

Abba, Father, all things are possible unto thee.
MARK 14:36 KJV

....
....
....
....
....
....
....
....
....
....
....
....
....
....
....
....
....
....

Receiving Jesus

Lord, I believe in Your name. Help me every day to believe still more. Take away the doubts and insecurities that the world shouts at me every day. Keep my eyes firmly focused on You, even when troubles come. Keep my ears attuned to Your voice, especially when I am tempted to listen to other voices. I welcome You into my heart—to make a home there now and forever.

But as many as received him, to them gave he power to become the sons of God, even to them that believe on his name.
JOHN 1:12 KJV

....
....
....
....
....
....
....
....
....
....
....
....
....
....
....
....
....
....

Good Gifts

Lord, You are good. You are good! You are a loving, generous God, slow to anger and rich in love. I pray that the riches You offer through Christ Jesus would be visible in my life, so that others would be drawn to You. I have nothing to offer them except You, Jesus. But You have so much, and You long to open the storehouses of heaven to us, blessings pressed down and running over. Amen.

*"If you then, being evil, know how to give good gifts to your children,
how much more will your Father who is in heaven give
what is good to those who ask Him!"*
MATTHEW 7:11 NASB

....
....
....
....
....
....
....
....
....
....
....
....
....
....
....
....
....

Lights

Lord, I am grateful that I can claim You as my Father. Because You live in my heart, I am Your representative to the world around me. Thank You for using me for Your purpose, and thank You for filling in the gaps where I am inadequate to do Your work. Make me Your light in the world around me, not so I can gain fame for myself but only to proclaim Your awesomeness.

That ye may be blameless and harmless, the sons of God,
without rebuke, in the midst of a crooked and perverse nation,
among whom ye shine as lights in the world.
PHILIPPIANS 2:15 KJV

....
....
....
....
....
....
....
....
....
....
....
....
....
....
....
....
....

Children of the Resurrection

Because I am Your child, I don't need to be afraid of death. You Yourself conquered death and the grave on Easter morning, and You promise me that Your grace will save me from eternal death as well. How amazing and wonderful and humbling! I am so glad, Lord, for the promise of Your resurrection and the assurance of eternity with You in heaven. Help me to be bold in sharing this wonderful hope with people who have no hope.

*Neither can they die any more: for they are. . .
the children of God, being the children of the resurrection.*
LUKE 20:36 KJV

....
....
....
....
....
....
....
....
....
....
....
....
....
....
....
....
....
....
....

The Missing "P"

Dear Father, today I just want to praise You! I spend so much time repenting (read: *sinning*), asking (complaining), and yielding (pretending not to be so stubborn), and so little time telling You how much I love You. You are merciful, You are awesome, You are holy! You are beyond compare. You are my Maker and sustainer. You saved me! You are light and love and all that is good. Lord, You made *mountains*. And trees that spear the clouds and birds as bright as rainbows and flowers as small and perfect as a baby's fingernail. Who is like You? Amen and amen and amen.

"For then you will delight in the Almighty and lift up your face to God."
JOB 22:26 NASB

....

....

....

....

....

....

....

....

....

....

....

....

....

....

....

....

....

Expecting Miracles

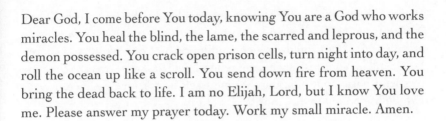

Dear God, I come before You today, knowing You are a God who works miracles. You heal the blind, the lame, the scarred and leprous, and the demon possessed. You crack open prison cells, turn night into day, and roll the ocean up like a scroll. You send down fire from heaven. You bring the dead back to life. I am no Elijah, Lord, but I know You love me. Please answer my prayer today. Work my small miracle. Amen.

Then the fire of the LORD fell and consumed the burnt sacrifice, and the wood and the stones and the dust, and it licked up the water that was in the trench.
1 KINGS 18:38 NKJV

....
....
....
....
....
....
....
....
....
....
....
....
....
....
....
....
....

Eating God's Holiness

Father, I honor Your name by taking my fill each day of Your holiness. Make Your Spirit alive and active in my heart today. Remind me to always seek You through prayer, meditation on Your Word, and simply being still in Your presence. And when I get "too busy" to take the time to spend with You, please invite me back into Your presence. I can't handle life on my own. . .nor do I want to.

That we might be partakers of his holiness.
HEBREWS 12:10 KJV

....
....
....
....
....
....
....
....
....
....
....
....
....
....
....
....
....
....

Light

Father God, Your name is light. You have no darkness in Your character. Your brilliance is dazzling—brighter than the brightest star and more beautiful than the most awe-inspiring celestial display. You are a hope-filled promise of never-ending illumination. Please shine on me—and shine *through* me so that others may see the darkness of this world flee before Your light.

> *God is light, and in him is no darkness at all.*
> 1 JOHN 1:5 KJV

....
....
....
....
....
....
....
....
....
....
....
....
....
....
....
....
....
....
....

More Than Just Talk

God, sometimes I talk a good game, but my heart and actions don't carry it through. Remind me that Your kingdom is active and powerful. It's not just a bunch of talk. It's real and it's here on earth now. You ask me to help build Your kingdom; show me new ways to serve. Give me a passion for Your kingdom on earth—and for Your heavenly kingdom as well.

For the kingdom of God is not in word, but in power.
1 CORINTHIANS 4:20 KJV

Who Holds the Reins?

Dear Father, I spend so much time trying to control others. Futilely. I feel my anxiety mounting, and I know that is not what You want. I can only control my own heart, Lord, and that is only because of Your grace and the gift of Your Spirit. I can't be the "holy spirit" of anyone else's heart. That is Your job. Please help me let go of my agenda and instead lift others up to You. Work on and through *me*, Lord, so they would be drawn closer to You. Amen.

All the ways of a man are pure in his own eyes, but the LORD weighs the spirits. Commit your works to the LORD, and your thoughts will be established.
PROVERBS 16:2–3 NKJV

....
....
....
....
....
....
....
....
....
....
....
....
....
....
....
....
....
....

God's Riches

Why should I ever doubt Your ability to give me what I need, heavenly Father, when You have such riches? Your bounty is unfathomable, and You want to share it with me! How humbling! Help me to remember that everything I call "mine" is actually Yours. Forgive me when my heart is hard and unwilling to accept Your riches in glory. Help me to be open to Your Spirit as He moves in my heart.

My God shall supply all your need according to his riches in glory by Christ Jesus.
PHILIPPIANS 4:19 KJV

....
....
....
....
....
....
....
....
....
....
....
....
....
....
....
....
....
....

No Wants

Since You are looking out for me—guarding and guiding me—I have everything I need. You are the Good Shepherd who supplies everything to me, Your sheep. Remind me every day that as a sheep, I cannot see the bigger picture—the dangers over the hill or the blessings that are mine to find. Help me more fully trust the Shepherd and His plans for me. Give me a heart of gratitude and a spirit that relinquishes control. Thank You, Lord.

The Lord is my shepherd; I shall not want.
PSALM 23:1 KJV

....
....
....
....
....
....
....
....
....
....
....
....
....
....
....
....
....
....

Seed and Bread

God, You aren't just a sower or a harvester; You're a true farmer. First You plant the seed; then You water it and nurture it, giving me the food and encouragement I need to grow in You. You work tirelessly to reap a bountiful harvest when my heart is full of fertile soil. I want to return the harvest to You, bearing beautiful fruits of righteousness. Keep working on me, farmer God—I am willing.

Now he that ministereth seed to the sower both minister bread for your food, and multiply your seed sown, and increase the fruits of your righteousness.
2 CORINTHIANS 9:10 KJV

....
....
....
....
....
....
....
....
....
....
....
....
....
....
....
....
....
....
....

Like Birds

Lord, if You keep track of the lives of birds, then I know I can trust You to watch over my own life. May I rest in the knowledge that You are always looking after me. I know I am worth much more to You than a bird. And even though I know I don't deserve it, I thank You for Your unconditional love.

Consider the ravens: for they neither sow nor reap;
which neither have storehouse nor barn; and God feedeth them:
how much more are ye better than the fowls?
LUKE 12:24 KJV

....
....
....
....
....
....
....
....
....
....
....
....
....
....
....
....
....
....

The Inspirational Word

Lord, Your Word thrills me, convicts me, comforts me, and strengthens me. I am so thankful that You gave us the Bible. Thank You for inspiring the prophets of old as they penned Your truth. Thank You for protecting the scripture through centuries of skepticism and persecution. Thank You for giving me the blessing of this treasure, for allowing me to hold it in my hand. When I am hungry, Your Word feeds me; when I am fearful, it assures me; when I am uncertain, it guides me. Your Book is the light upon my path. Without it, I would be lost. Amen.

All Scripture is God-breathed and is useful for teaching, rebuking, correcting and training in righteousness.
2 Timothy 3:16 niv

....
....
....
....
....
....
....
....
....
....
....
....
....
....
....
....

Prayer and Thanksgiving

Even while I'm asking You for something, Lord, I can already thank You. I know You hear my prayers and will answer with "Yes," "No," or "Wait." Thank You for often taking care of my needs even before I ask. What a comfort it is that You already know what I need. I can trust You absolutely to answer me in the best way and according to Your purpose.

Be careful for nothing; but in every thing by prayer and supplication with thanksgiving let your requests be made known unto God.
PHILIPPIANS 4:6 KJV

....
....
....
....
....
....
....
....
....
....
....
....
....
....
....
....
....
....

To Every Generation

Jehovah God, I come just now to revel in Your faithfulness. From generations past to this very minute, multitudes have testified that You always come through. Yet there have been times in my life when I thought You had overlooked me, that You weren't aware of my needs, that You didn't hear my prayers. But my doubts proved false, and Your record is untarnished. You didn't promise that I would always understand Your ways, but You did promise Your presence and love in every circumstance. And I can testify it's true. I love You, Lord. Amen.

Your faithfulness endures to all generations.
PSALM 119:90 NKJV

....
....
....
....
....
....
....
....
....
....
....
....
....
....
....
....
....
....
....

Brighter

Dear good, gracious heavenly Father, sometimes it is so dark here. Not just the darkness of night or storm or interiors: the darkness of sin and unknowing presses close. I am reaching up for Your light in the only way I can. Thank You, Lord, for Your Word. It comforts and illuminates in a way that nothing else does. It makes You present and real to me. I praise You for giving me something that is so *alive* with Your Spirit to be my anchor and lantern in the darkness. Amen.

The entrance and unfolding of Your words give light; their unfolding gives understanding (discernment and comprehension) to the simple.
PSALM 119:130 AMPC

....
....
....
....
....
....
....
....
....
....
....
....
....
....
....
....
....

Tomorrow

The truth is that I have no control over tomorrow, Lord. Free me from worries about the future, whether tomorrow or next week or next year. May I rely on You today, so that I can focus on the here and now, this moment, and trust You to take care of whatever comes next. I do trust You, Father. Help my actions be evidence to that fact. I yearn for the freedom that comes from being worry-free!

Take therefore no thought for the morrow: for the morrow shall take thought for the things of itself.
MATTHEW 6:34 KJV

....
....
....
....
....
....
....
....
....
....
....
....
....
....
....
....
....
....

The Past Is Gone

Father, I'm glad You have redeemed my past. I've said and done things of which I'm not proud. I'm grateful that You've blotted out my sins and given me a fresh start. Like one using a marker board, You wiped away the shame and guilt and handed the marker back to me. I don't have to live in the past; I can face the future with confidence and grace. In Christ's name, amen.

As far as the east is from the west, so far has
He removed our transgressions from us.
PSALM 103:12 NKJV

....
....
....
....
....
....
....
....
....
....
....
....
....
....
....
....
....
....

Weeds

Dear Lord, You are the master Gardener. I love to plant flowers, vegetables, bushes, and bulbs, but nothing in my garden can compare with the glory that was Eden. My garden is nothing like that perfection: if I ignore it for two weeks, weeds spring up; in two months it would be a jungle. My life is just like my garden, Lord. Sometimes new things seem insignificant at first: a new TV program, a new book, a new acquaintance, a new train of thought. But they can grow rampantly. Give me wisdom to recognize weeds when they are small and pluck them out. Amen.

For wisdom is better than rubies, and all the things
one may desire cannot be compared with her.
PROVERBS 8:11 NKJV

....
....
....
....
....
....
....
....
....
....
....
....
....
....
....
....
....

Watered

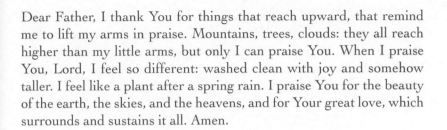

Dear Father, I thank You for things that reach upward, that remind me to lift my arms in praise. Mountains, trees, clouds: they all reach higher than my little arms, but only I can praise You. When I praise You, Lord, I feel so different: washed clean with joy and somehow taller. I feel like a plant after a spring rain. I praise You for the beauty of the earth, the skies, and the heavens, and for Your great love, which surrounds and sustains it all. Amen.

He dawns on them like the morning light when the sun rises on a cloudless morning, when the tender grass springs out of the earth through clear shining after rain.
2 SAMUEL 23:4 AMPC

....
....
....
....
....
....
....
....
....
....
....
....
....
....
....
....
....

Promises

Jesus' blood is the new testament—the new promise You have made to me, Lord. I am not bound by the rules and regulations of the Old Testament law, but instead I have been given amazing freedom! The blood of Jesus is so powerful that I cannot comprehend it, but please help me to always rely on His saving blood that heals all my sins.

This is my blood of the new testament,
which is shed for many for the remission of sins.
MATTHEW 26:28 KJV

....
....
....
....
....
....
....
....
....
....
....
....
....
....
....
....
....
....

Hungry Souls

God, my soul gets so hungry for You sometimes. I know that it's not You who has moved away, but the problem is with me. Thank You that You are immovable, unshakable, and always there. Because of this, I know just where to run to find You, to satisfy my longing soul. Give me a firm footing in Your presence so I am not tempted to wander away again. Thank You for being patient with me.

For he satisfieth the longing soul, and filleth the hungry soul with goodness.
PSALM 107:9 KJV

....
....
....
....
....
....
....
....
....
....
....
....
....
....
....
....
....
....
....

Rich in Grace

The world tells me I should be rich in material wealth, Father, but true riches are found in Your limitless grace. Thank You for the richness of Your grace, Lord. Thank You that Your grace is large enough to cover all my past sin, my current sin, and my future sin. That's the kind of rich inheritance I truly desire!

In whom we have redemption through his blood,
the forgiveness of sins, according to the riches of his grace.
EPHESIANS 1:7 KJV

....
....
....
....
....
....
....
....
....
....
....
....
....
....
....
....
....
....
....

Fitness

It's an exercise-crazy world we live in, Lord. Gym memberships are prized, morning jogs are eulogized, and workout clothing has become a fashion statement. There are some who make this area of self-care too important; they spend an inordinate amount of time on it. Yet others don't keep it high enough on their priority list. Help me, God, to keep the proper perspective of fitness, because, after all, I have a responsibility for the upkeep on this body. It's on loan from You. Amen.

"Physical training is good, but training for godliness is much better, promising benefits in this life and in the life to come."
1 TIMOTHY 4:8 NLT

....
....
....
....
....
....
....
....
....
....
....
....
....
....
....
....
....
....

Unlimited Resources

Father, the Bible says You own "the cattle on a thousand hills." You have unlimited resources. So I'm asking You to supply a special need I have today. Although I try to be a good steward of the money You give me, some unexpected event has caught me without the necessary funds. I know You can remedy this situation, if You deem that good for me. Because You're my Father, I'm asking for Your financial advice. I need Your wisdom in this area of my life. Amen.

"For every animal of the forest is mine, and the cattle on a thousand hills."
PSALM 50:10 NIV

....

....

....

....

....

....

....

....

....

....

....

....

....

....

....

....

....

....

God's Children

Brothers and sisters often bicker and squabble. My siblings and I are no exception. But remind me, dear God, that Your children should be following You, not fighting with each other. Grant us an abundance of grace when we are dealing with each other, and help us keep our eyes solely on You as we work through difficulties. If we are following Your will, we will be blessed beyond imagination.

Be ye therefore followers of God, as dear children.
EPHESIANS 5:1 KJV

....
....
....
....
....
....
....
....
....
....
....
....
....
....
....
....
....
....

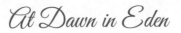

At Dawn in Eden

Dear Father, I have always longed to be in the Garden of Eden in those first days when You walked with Adam and Eve in the cool of the day. You enjoyed Your creation; You thought it was beautiful. You enjoyed Your creatures, especially Your people, and You wanted to spend time with them. I am so sorry for what we lost, and I know You are, too. We lost the completeness we had in Eden: we lost that perfect garden and that perfect fellowship with You. But the gift is not like the trespass. Thank You that what You gave us in Jesus Christ is even more beautiful than what we lost. Amen.

And they heard the sound of the Lord God
walking in the garden in the cool of the day.
Genesis 3:8 nkjv

....

....

....

....

....

....

....

....

....

....

....

....

....

....

....

Shielded

Lord, You tell me that my faith is a shield that will protect me from evil. Right now I ask You to reinforce that shield. Give me a greater, stronger faith so that I will be ready when I go through difficult times, when Satan is shooting his fiery darts directly at me. I will not live in fear about this possibility, but I will stand on Your promises.

Above all, taking the shield of faith, wherewith ye
shall be able to quench all the fiery darts of the wicked.
EPHESIANS 6:16 KJV

....
....
....
....
....
....
....
....
....
....
....
....
....
....
....
....
....
....
....

The Already-Done List

Dear God, I love plans and schedules. They help me stay focused and productive and turn the 1,440 minutes in each day into goals set and attained. But I know I have missed opportunities to deepen relationships because I was too busy checking off boxes on my to-do list or too rigid to change plans at the last minute. And I know that often I base my idea of how much *I* am worth on how much I have been able to accomplish. Help me remember that I can never *do* enough to earn Your love. I am already loved, completely and eternally. The only thing that really needed doing, You did on the cross. Thank You, Lord.

"I have loved you with an everlasting love;
therefore I have drawn you with lovingkindness."
JEREMIAH 31:3 NASB

....

....

....

....

....

....

....

....

....

....

....

....

....

....

....

....

God's Armor

Father, remind me not to venture out into life's temptations and trials without first putting on Your armor, especially the breastplate of faith and love and the helmet of Your salvation. Teach me to grab hold of these gifts and harness the power that You offer through them. Give me the opportunity to use these pieces of armor to bless others, protecting them against the power of evil.

But let us, who are of the day, be sober, putting on the breastplate
of faith and love; and for an helmet, the hope of salvation.
1 THESSALONIANS 5:8 KJV

....

....

....

....

....

....

....

....

....

....

....

....

....

....

....

....

....

God's Gentleness

Father God, when I think about Your gift of salvation to me, I think about the mighty work that Your grace through the death of Jesus Christ does in my life. But there's another side to it. God, thank You for Your gentleness that makes me strong enough to rise above every trial that comes my way. It's because I am saved that I can be free to stand and not be afraid.

Thou hast also given me the shield of thy salvation:
and thy gentleness hath made me great.
2 SAMUEL 22:36 KJV

....
....
....
....
....
....
....
....
....
....
....
....
....
....
....
....
....

A Quiet Quest

Dear Lord, we all find great blessings when in the company of others, enjoying those times when we are with people. But I need Your help to embrace solitude, too. Let me see the value in spending some time alone, giving my mind time to decompress, refreshing my spirit in the quiet. Not only do I need to spend quiet time with You in personal worship, but I also need to incorporate into my daily routine those pockets of time when the music is off and the computer is down. Help me make times of quiet my quest. Amen.

"In quietness and confidence shall be your strength."
ISAIAH 30:15 NKJV

....
....
....
....
....
....
....
....
....
....
....
....
....
....
....
....
....

Lit

When everywhere I look I see only darkness, please, Lord, turn on the lights in my heart. Show me ways to share that illumination with everyone around me. When Your light burns, darkness flees. Use me. Light me, I pray.

Let your loins be girded about, and your lights burning.
LUKE 12:35 KJV

....
....
....
....
....
....
....
....
....
....
....
....
....
....
....
....
....
....
....
....
....
....

Delivered

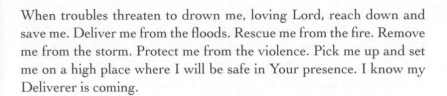

When troubles threaten to drown me, loving Lord, reach down and save me. Deliver me from the floods. Rescue me from the fire. Remove me from the storm. Protect me from the violence. Pick me up and set me on a high place where I will be safe in Your presence. I know my Deliverer is coming.

Because he hath set his love upon me, therefore will I deliver him:
I will set him on high, because he hath known my name.
PSALM 91:14 KJV

....
....
....
....
....
....
....
....
....
....
....
....
....
....
....
....
....
....

The Liar

Dear God, someone I care about told me a lie today—in church, no less. It was a small lie, about an insignificant thing, but it felt like a brick had been thrown at me. I carried that brick like an ugly goblin baby—a changeling—all through the service, and the music, the sermon, the fellowship of other believers were soured for me because of my burden. Then I realized, Lord, because You so lovingly showed me, that the burden had become mine because I chose to carry it. Thank You for showing me how to lay that ugly thing at the foot of the cross and pick up joy instead. Amen.

If we confess our sins, he is faithful and just to forgive us our sins,
and to cleanse us from all unrighteousness.
1 JOHN 1:9 KJV

....

....

....

....

....

....

....

....

....

....

....

....

....

....

....

Alive and Blessed

Sickness. . .violence. . .exhaustion. . .stress: our world is full of dangers. Some of the dangers I face are truly life threatening, Lord. But I don't want to live a life of fear. You call me to be bold and fearless. Thank You that You've promised to not only save my life but also to bless me.

The LORD will preserve him, and keep him alive; and he shall be blessed upon the earth: and thou wilt not deliver him unto the will of his enemies.
PSALM 41:2 KJV

....

....

....

....

....

....

....

....

....

....

....

....

....

....

....

....

....

....

....

....

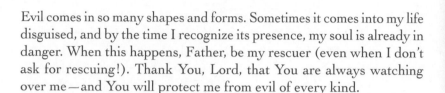

Saved from All Evil

Evil comes in so many shapes and forms. Sometimes it comes into my life disguised, and by the time I recognize its presence, my soul is already in danger. When this happens, Father, be my rescuer (even when I don't ask for rescuing!). Thank You, Lord, that You are always watching over me—and You will protect me from evil of every kind.

The LORD shall preserve thee from all evil: he shall preserve thy soul.
PSALM 121:7 KJV

....
....
....
....
....
....
....
....
....
....
....
....
....
....
....
....
....
....
....

Never Forsaken

Father God, I've experienced abandonment in my life. The experience left me feeling empty, alone, helpless. Thank You, Father, that You will never forsake me; You will never abandon me. I am grateful for the security this promise affords me. You will keep me safe forever in Your loving arms that are big enough and strong enough to hold me and all my issues.

For the LORD loveth judgment, and forsaketh
not his saints; they are preserved for ever.
PSALM 37:28 KJV

....
....
....
....
....
....
....
....
....
....
....
....
....
....
....
....
....
....

Just Do It

Dear Lord, I want to have an obedient heart. Sometimes, when You speak to me, I feel hesitation or want to postpone what You're telling me to do. Yet that means either I don't trust You or I want my own way, neither of which is good. A child ought to obey her parents because she acknowledges their right to direct her and because she trusts the love behind the words. Help me, Lord, to embrace that kind of attitude when You speak to me. In Christ's name, amen.

But be doers of the word, and not hearers only, deceiving yourselves.
JAMES 1:22 NKJV

....
....
....
....
....
....
....
....
....
....
....
....
....
....
....
....
....
....

True Homeland Perspective

God, I want to live with an eternal perspective. Heaven is more than a feel-good fable for the graveside. It's an actual place, as real as this earth and far more lasting. When I live like this earth is the ultimate goal, I tend toward selfish indulgence. When I remember that heaven is my real destination, I put value on the lasting things, the things of true importance. Remind me to keep an eye toward Your heavenly kingdom.

They agreed that they were foreigners and nomads here on earth.
Obviously people who say such things are looking forward
to a country they can call their own.
HEBREWS 11:13–14 NLT

....
....
....
....
....
....
....
....
....
....
....
....
....
....
....
....
....

My Hiding Place

Heavenly Father, when the world seems like a dangerous place, when anxieties rush at me everywhere I turn, be my hiding place. Be by my side and let me run into Your arms. Wrap me up in Your embrace and sing to me Your sweet song of deliverance. May I never think I'm so self-sufficient that I reject Your comfort and protection, Daddy.

Thou art my hiding place; thou shalt preserve me from trouble;
thou shalt compass me about with songs of deliverance.
PSALM 32:7 KJV

....
....
....
....
....
....
....
....
....
....
....
....
....
....
....
....
....
....
....

The Simple Life

Dear God, *simplicity* is a buzzword today. It seems everyone wants "simple" in some fashion. Perhaps it's because life has become too complicated for many of us; we yearn for a more laid-back lifestyle. Lord, I need to simplify my goals in my relationships and my work. Doing so will help me to have a more laser-like focus. And in my spiritual life, a little simplifying might be good, too. Instead of daily reading numerous chapters of Your Word, help me to concentrate on one or two verses, thus deepening my understanding of You. Lord, help me keep simple goals and a simple faith as I simply live for You. Amen.

Aspire to lead a quiet life, to mind your own business,
and to work with your own hands.
1 Thessalonians 4:11 nkjv

....
....
....
....
....
....
....
....
....
....
....
....
....
....
....
....

Mirror, Mirror

Father, when I look at certain people I know, all I see is how much I lack in comparison. They seem naturally kinder, more at ease, more fashionable, more attractive, and certainly thinner. I know, Lord, I often spend more time thinking about how other people see me than about how You see me. You made me, sovereign Lord, in this particular way for Your purposes. Help me trust You, and trust that this lump of clay that You are molding is precious in Your sight and in Your hands. Amen.

I will praise You, for I am fearfully and wonderfully made.
PSALM 139:14 NKJV

....
....
....
....
....
....
....
....
....
....
....
....
....
....
....
....
....
....

My Refuge

In times of trouble, Lord, when I feel that the pressure is overwhelming, thank You that You are my Refuge—a place of peace, love, and acceptance. Teach me to seek Your protection at the onset of troubles, rather than trying to handle them on my own. I don't get extra points for trying to stick it out by myself.

The LORD also will be a refuge for the oppressed, a refuge in times of trouble.
PSALM 9:9 KJV

....
....
....
....
....
....
....
....
....
....
....
....
....
....
....
....
....
....
....
....
....

Singing

God, You know all the troubles that surround me—but today, I'm going to start my day singing. Give me a song of power and mercy that will stay with me all day long, especially when the stresses of the day come. No matter what life throws at me, I want to live with Your joyful melody in my heart until Jesus returns to take me home!

But I will sing of thy power; yea, I will sing aloud of thy mercy in the morning: for thou hast been my defence and refuge in the day of my trouble.
PSALM 59:16 KJV

....
....
....
....
....
....
....
....
....
....
....
....
....
....
....
....
....
....

Hope

God, I know that one of the surest ways to find Your hope is to open up scripture and meditate on Your Word. There I learn that You thought of me at the beginning of creation, that You formed me in my mother's womb, that You love me and cherish me, that You provided a way for me to have an intimate relationship with You through the death, burial, and resurrection of Jesus Christ, and that You have amazing plans for me here and into eternity. Your words fill me with amazing hope, Father.

Thou art my hiding place and my shield: I hope in thy word.
PSALM 119:114 KJV

....
....
....
....
....
....
....
....
....
....
....
....
....
....
....
....
....
....

My Prayer Warriors

I thank You, Lord, today for all the people who have prayed for me. I am humbled by how I have been surrounded, from the day I was born, by people who have lifted me up to the throne of grace, faithfully and passionately. I may not ever know who they are, but I ask You to bless them today. Strengthen their faith in the invisible power of their work. I ask that You would bring me to their minds today, Lord, for I covet their intercession. Thank You for these faithful warriors. I need them so desperately. Amen.

Always labouring fervently for you in prayers, that ye may stand perfect and complete in all the will of God.
COLOSSIANS 4:12 KJV

....
....
....
....
....
....
....
....
....
....
....
....
....
....
....
....

Yes and No

God, teach me Your ways so that no evil will take root in my life. Remind me to make my word count, so that my "yes" means yes, and my "no" means no. Make me a person of integrity that others can trust. When people ask me why I do what I do, let me always point them to You.

But let your communication be, Yea, yea; Nay, nay:
for whatsoever is more than these cometh of evil.
MATTHEW 5:37 KJV

....
....
....
....
....
....
....
....
....
....
....
....
....
....
....
....
....
....
....

Back to Center

Heavenly Father, I need balance in my life. It's one of the hardest things for humans to achieve. We're so prone to lopsidedness, to extremes. Maintaining center is challenging. That's why I need You to straighten me out and help me stay in the narrow way. In those areas of my life where I'm listing to the side, bring me back to center, O Lord. In Jesus' name, amen.

Mark out a straight path for your feet so that those who are weak and lame will not fall but become strong.
HEBREWS 12:13 NLT

....
....
....
....
....
....
....
....
....
....
....
....
....
....
....
....
....
....
....

Hospitality

Dear Lord, I need to improve my skills in hospitality. Because You have blessed me, I need to share with others. In fact, hospitality is one of those virtues the apostle Paul commanded of the church. Sharing my home with others is my Christian duty and also a great way to reach out to unbelievers I have befriended. Please let me not dread hosting others but rather find ways to make it doable and enjoyable for all. In Jesus' name, amen.

Use hospitality one to another without grudging.
1 PETER 4:9 KJV

....
....
....
....
....
....
....
....
....
....
....
....
....
....
....
....
....
....

Firm

God, I know You are faithful. Be my Rock and my firm foothold, and please be the foundation of my life. Make me firm and solid, so that I can always resist evil. When my own faith is firmly rooted, then please allow me to help others find their strength in Your faithfulness. Your strength will sustain all Your children!

But the Lord is faithful, who shall stablish you, and keep you from evil.
2 THESSALONIANS 3:3 KJV

....
....
....
....
....
....
....
....
....
....
....
....
....
....
....
....
....
....
....
....

No Slipping

I'm coming to a situation in my life where the way ahead looks slippery and dangerous, Lord. Please hold my hand, and when necessary pick me up and carry me. I know that You won't leave me or even take a break to get a little rest. Thank You that I can rest in You, even during difficult stretches of the path.

He will not suffer thy foot to be moved: he that keepeth thee will not slumber.
PSALM 121:3 KJV

....
....
....
....
....
....
....
....
....
....
....
....
....
....
....
....
....
....
....
....

Straight Ways

God, You know how hard it is for me sometimes to know which way I should go. Today I ask that You be my map and my guide. Please show me clearly the way You want me to follow. Remind me that You've already "been there and done that." While I may question why we're going a certain way, You know what is best, and You have great plans for me.

Lead me, O LORD, in thy righteousness because of mine enemies;
make thy way straight before my face.
PSALM 5:8 KJV

....

....

....

....

....

....

....

....

....

....

....

....

....

....

....

....

....

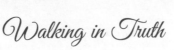

Walking in Truth

I am guilty of having a divided heart, God. I want to do Your will, but I also want my will to be done. Forgive me for my selfishness. When my heart feels torn with conflicting desires, Father God, please unite me, so that I have a single focus in life: Your way, Your truth, Your will, Your path.

Teach me thy way, O LORD; I will walk in thy truth:
unite my heart to fear thy name.
PSALM 86:11 KJV

....
....
....
....
....
....
....
....
....
....
....
....
....
....
....
....
....
....

Cobwebs of the Soul

Dear Father, You know how good I feel when my house is in order, when the floors are swept, the bathrooms are clean, the beds are made, and the toys are picked up. It imparts an order and peace to my soul. And You know how I feel when chaos reigns: scattered, bewildered, short tempered. Help me remember that it is no different with my spiritual house. Help me keep the cobwebs and confusion in check with daily prayer, study, and meditation on Your Word. And thank You that I *can*. Amen.

You will keep him in perfect peace, whose mind is stayed on You.
ISAIAH 26:3 NKJV

....
....
....
....
....
....
....
....
....
....
....
....
....
....
....
....
....

Friends for Every Need

Dear heavenly Father, I am grateful for my friends. They are such a vital part of my life. When my family can't be there, my friends come through for me. When I need someone to gripe to, they will listen. When I need a kick to get me going again, they don't hesitate. My journey through life would be so lonely and unhappy without these amazing women who walk it with me. Thank You for blessing me through them. Help me return the favor. Amen.

A time to weep, and a time to laugh; a time to mourn, and a time to dance.
ECCLESIASTES 3:4 NKJV

God's Eye

I have a dog that follows the direction of my gaze and knows what I want her to do. All I need to do is look at her bed for her to go there and lie down; if I look in another direction, toward a treat I've hidden for her, she leaps up and runs to the morsel of food. Lord, help me to be as responsive to Your gaze. Keep me so tuned in to You that You can use Your eyes to show me where You want me to go.

I will instruct thee and teach thee in the way
which thou shalt go: I will guide thee with mine eye.
PSALM 32:8 KJV

....
....
....
....
....
....
....
....
....
....
....
....
....
....
....
....
....
....

For My Own Good

Sometimes I forget, Lord, that Your guidance is always for my good. I admit that sometimes it feels a little bit like taking my medicine. But You want what's truly best for me. Your paths always lead me to joy and blessing and health. Teach me to trust You more fully today and every day.

Thus saith the LORD, thy Redeemer, the Holy One of Israel;
I am the LORD thy God which teacheth thee to profit,
which leadeth thee by the way that thou shouldest go.
ISAIAH 48:17 KJV

....
....
....
....
....
....
....
....
....
....
....
....
....
....
....
....
....

The Proof Is in the Pudding

Dear Father, we are a gullible people. From the very beginning, we were tricked and led astray. Satan whispered in Eve's ear, she listened, and everyone ever since has been falling for his lies. *Just this once. It doesn't really matter. I deserve this. No one will find out.* We believe his lies about everything from eating too much chocolate, to "borrowing" a pencil from work, to committing adultery or murder. I am no different. I need You every moment, Lord, to help me sort through the chatter in my head so I can be certain what to listen to and what to stand against. Only the truth. Only what glorifies You. Amen.

"Then you will know the truth, and the truth will set you free."
JOHN 8:32 NIV

....
....
....
....
....
....
....
....
....
....
....
....
....
....
....
....

The Path of Life

Why do I think I'm a trailblazer, Lord? Sometimes my way seems better to me, so I take a little side trip off Your path, only to find disappointment, destruction, and heartbreak. I know that only Your path, God, leads me to life. . .to joy. . .to pleasures that will last forever. I will put blinders on my eyes, Father—looking straight ahead to You.

Thou wilt shew me the path of life: in thy presence is fulness of joy;
at thy right hand there are pleasures for evermore.
PSALM 16:11 KJV

....
....
....
....
....
....
....
....
....
....
....
....
....
....
....
....
....
....
....

Faithful Friendship

Father, I need to confront my friend. She seems to be making some bad decisions. I'm so afraid for her. Please keep me from joining in the discussions of others who are talking about her. Yet my just being silent isn't what she needs. I know some things about her life that have brought her to today; I know her secret pain and longings. Let me not betray her but rather come alongside to share the burden she's carrying, and perhaps lovingly suggest another solution than the one she's trying. Heal her heart, Lord, and give me guidance in the process. In Christ's name, amen.

Faithful are the wounds of a friend.
PROVERBS 27:6 NKJV

....
....
....
....
....
....
....
....
....
....
....
....
....
....
....
....
....

Everlasting Ways

You know, Lord God, how easily I hide selfishness inside my heart. But try as I might, I cannot hide it from You. Shine Your light on all my blind spots. Show me where I need to grow and change to be more like You. Bring true godly friends into my life that can help me in these areas. Lead me in the path that will lead me to eternity.

See if there be any wicked way in me, and lead me in the way everlasting.
PSALM 139:24 KJV

....
....
....
....
....
....
....
....
....
....
....
....
....
....
....
....
....
....
....
....

Instructions in Righteousness

Lord, I want to thank You for this verse in Matthew. When You tell us to pray for our enemies (or even those we're just annoyed with), it works. I quite literally can't hold on to my negative feelings about a person when I'm lifting them up to You. Your Word is powerful, and, when I obey it, I feel Your power at work in me. When I feel crushed by the weight of unforgiveness, like I don't have a hope or a prayer, this verse offers me both: it gives me a specific prayer to pray and tells what will happen if I do. I want to be Your child. Thank You for showing me how. Amen.

"But I tell you, love your enemies and pray for those who persecute you, that you may be children of your Father in heaven."
MATTHEW 5:44–45 NIV

....
....
....
....
....
....
....
....
....
....
....
....
....
....
....
....

Eternal

When I think about eternity, God, I realize that the time I spend on earth is pretty insignificant. But I still get so focused on my daily problems, Lord, that they seem insurmountable. Burdens and worries eat away at my joy, Lord. Instead, I choose to yield myself to whatever comes into my life and rely on Your power to get me through. Use my problems and troubles to transform me for eternity, I pray.

For our light affliction, which is but for a moment, worketh for us a far more exceeding and eternal weight of glory.
2 CORINTHIANS 4:17 KJV

....
....
....
....
....
....
....
....
....
....
....
....
....
....
....
....
....

Not Good Enough

Father, shopping for clothing at the mall makes me so insecure. The store windows are filled with posters of glamorous women in size 0 clothing. I feel I will never "measure up" to these airbrushed supermodels. Like every other twenty-first-century woman I know, I struggle with body image. Although these feelings of inferiority seem petty, and a bit self-centered, they are so real sometimes that I get depressed. I know that isn't what You want for me. Help me with these feelings and show me the way to triumph over them. In Christ's name, amen.

I praise you because I am fearfully and wonderfully made.
PSALM 139:14 NIV

....
....
....
....
....
....
....
....
....
....
....
....
....
....
....
....
....
....
....
....

Blessed Hope

Some days, Father, I hold on to a single thread of hope. But the hope You offer through Jesus Christ is real and active, and even when it's wearing thin, it sustains me. The hope I have in You, God, is for the future—but it blesses me today. Fortify my hope so that I can share it with other weary travelers in this world. Help me direct them to the true source of hope.

Looking for that blessed hope, and the glorious appearing of the great God and our Saviour Jesus Christ.
Titus 2:13 KJV

....
....
....
....
....
....
....
....
....
....
....
....
....
....
....
....
....
....

Future Glory

When it comes down to it, God, it's not all about me. I am guilty of being so selfish, self-centered, "me focused" that I lose perspective of the big picture. Father God, when pain surrounds me, give me a glimpse of the glory that lies ahead. Help me regain a proper sense of perspective. Show me where You want me in Your will!

For I reckon that the sufferings of this present time are not worthy to be compared with the glory which shall be revealed in us.
ROMANS 8:18 KJV

....
....
....
....
....
....
....
....
....
....
....
....
....
....
....
....
....
....
....

The Same Old Me

Lord, today I come to You a bit discouraged. The traits I see in myself are ones I don't like. It seems I could do much more for You without some of the inherent flaws of my personality. So help me overcome my defects, or please use me in spite of them. Help me love myself, as imperfect as I am, and strive to be the best me I can be. I know You can find a way around my impediments and use me for Your glory, just like You used Moses in spite of his speech problem. Amen.

You have searched me, Lord, and you know me.
PSALM 139:1 NIV

....
....
....
....
....
....
....
....
....
....
....
....
....
....
....
....
....
....

Timely Wisdom

Lord, I wasted my time this afternoon watching a movie. I needed to do other things, but I got caught up in the plot. Now I'm running behind in my schedule. Thank You, Lord, for giving writers and moviemakers the gifts necessary to craft moving stories, sometimes life-changing dramas. But help me to use my time more wisely so I can enjoy this pleasure sans guilt. And, Lord, help me to guard my mind carefully when I'm selecting what to watch. Amen.

For the LORD gives wisdom; from His
mouth come knowledge and understanding.
PROVERBS 2:6 NKJV

....
....
....
....
....
....
....
....
....
....
....
....
....
....
....
....
....
....

The Power of Words

Father, my mouth sometimes gets me into trouble. Please keep me aware of the things I say that aren't right. Let me back up and apologize if I've hurt anyone. Better yet, let me consider my words before I cast them out on the wind. Once spoken, they can never be recalled. Your written Word is living, brilliant, and powerful; Jesus is the embodiment of it—the Living Word. My spoken earthly words are weighty as well; they can minister life or death to those who hear. I ask You to remind me of this throughout the day. Amen.

Death and life are in the power of the tongue:
and they that love it shall eat the fruit thereof.
PROVERBS 18:21 KJV

....
....
....
....
....
....
....
....
....
....
....
....
....
....
....
....
....

God's Thoughts

God, You know how easily my thoughts turn to worries and fears. Teach me to think Your thoughts instead: thoughts of peace and goodness that will lead me into the future You have planned for me. Show me the steps I should take to reach the abundant life You have in store for me, both here on earth and in eternity.

For I know the thoughts that I think toward you, saith the LORD, thoughts of peace, and not of evil, to give you an expected end.
JEREMIAH 29:11 KJV

....
....
....
....
....
....
....
....
....
....
....
....
....
....
....
....
....
....

The Missing Link

Dear Lord, sometimes I have to laugh at how hard people work to explain life apart from a Creator. They are desperate to throw their lot in with amoebas in a primordial soup pot rather than with a loving, creative God who might require something of them. But I thank You that You did create the universe out of nothing and us out of the dust of the earth. You spoke light into existence. Not in a billion years could we design a universe so complex, detailed, and interlocking. Thank You for the amazing love that keeps it all spinning. Amen.

Then God said, "Let there be light"; and there was light. God saw that the light was good; and God separated the light from the darkness.
GENESIS 1:3–4 NASB

....
....
....
....
....
....
....
....
....
....
....
....
....
....
....
....
....

Abundance

Father, I often put limits on what is possible in my life—to my own detriment! Help me recall the miracles You've done in my life—the "God incidents" that have Your fingerprints all over them. Remind me to share these fantastic stories with others so they too might learn to see You at work in their lives. Give me Your eyes to see the endless power You have at work in me. May I expect Your abundance to fill my future.

> *[God] is able to do exceeding abundantly above all that we ask or think, according to the power that worketh in us.*
> EPHESIANS 3:20 KJV

....
....
....
....
....
....
....
....
....
....
....
....
....
....
....
....
....
....
....

No Spirit of Fear

Father, I deal with a phobia. It isn't anything life threatening, but it's embarrassing. I haven't told anyone, and I'm hoping I never have to. But I ask You now to help me; I don't want my phobia to keep me from living the life You've planned for me. Help me to bring this fear to You; show me that You are in control, that You are the security system in my life. I ask this in Jesus' name, amen.

For God hath not given us the spirit of fear;
but of power, and of love, and of a sound mind.
2 Timothy 1:7 KJV

....
....
....
....
....
....
....
....
....
....
....
....
....
....
....
....
....
....

Pack Nothing but Faith

Dear Lord, Your world is so beautiful and *large*. Sometimes I sigh for all the places I will never see before I die. Mount Everest flying its white cloud-flag of spindrift. Greek islands floating in a wine-dark sea. A blue morpho flickering through the black-green-gold of the jungle. I miss them, somehow, though I've never seen them. But I know that nothing good will be lost, and I am confident that in heaven, I will ache for nothing left behind. I praise You for what *is* and for what will be. Amen.

Now faith is the assurance of things hoped for,
the conviction of things not seen.
HEBREWS 11:1 NASB

....
....
....
....
....
....
....
....
....
....
....
....
....
....
....
....
....
....
....
....

Obsidian

Lord, my house is full of the flu, but I praise You with a kind of wide-eyed joy. I feel *patience* (where did *that* come from?) thickening like a skin over the lava of my usual anger, and I know that it can only come from You. I walk gingerly, Lord, because I don't yet trust myself. Will I fall through? Is it thick enough to hold? But thank You for what You are slowly forming beneath my feet: solid rock. Amen.

> *The LORD liveth; and blessed be my rock;*
> *and exalted be the God of the rock of my salvation.*
> 2 SAMUEL 22:47 KJV

....
....
....
....
....
....
....
....
....
....
....
....
....
....
....
....
....

Shining More and More

Father, when I am in vibrant fellowship with You, the path before me seems clearer and Your will seems more evident. Thank You for the light that shines brighter with each step I take. When the light seems dim or I'm not sure which way to go, bring me back into Your presence and lead me to Your holy Word. Thank You for never giving up on me, Father.

The path of the just is as the shining light, that
shineth more and more unto the perfect day.
PROVERBS 4:18 KJV

....
....
....
....
....
....
....
....
....
....
....
....
....
....
....
....
....

Face-to-Face

You know that I can't see You clearly, Father. You know I don't really understand You, even when I am seeking You every day. I'm grateful, though, that I expect to see You face-to-face—and that on that day, I will finally truly know You even more intimately and personally than now. What an awe-inspiring promise!

For now we see through a glass, darkly; but then face to face:
now I know in part; but then shall I know even as also I am known.
1 CORINTHIANS 13:12 KJV

....
....
....
....
....
....
....
....
....
....
....
....
....
....
....
....
....
....

Coveting

God, it's so easy to break the tenth commandment: do not covet (see Exodus 20:17). Coveting is a way of life for many in our world. But You say we shouldn't compare ourselves with the "Joneses," nor envy them and what they have. Whatever You've given me is to be enjoyed and received, not held up for inspection. Teach me a deeper gratefulness for Your blessings. In Jesus' name, amen.

Let your conduct be without covetousness.
HEBREWS 13:5 NKJV

....
....
....
....
....
....
....
....
....
....
....
....
....
....
....
....
....
....
....

Joy

Some days, Lord, things are going so well that it feels like all of creation is singing Your praises, and I join with them. Other days, even when creation sings, I don't feel like praising. Thank You, Lord, for the reminder from the mountains and trees that no matter what today brings, You promise me joy. Help me live out Your joy every day.

For ye shall go out with joy, and be led forth with peace: the mountains and the hills shall break forth before you into singing, and all the trees of the field shall clap their hands.
ISAIAH 55:12 KJV

....
....
....
....
....
....
....
....
....
....
....
....
....
....
....
....
....
....

I Will Lift Up Mine Eyes

Lord, I praise You for mountains. I praise You for the old, rolling backs of the Appalachians. I praise You for the sharp, unworn spires of the Himalayas. I praise You for snowcapped peaks and glacier-grooved summits and the way mountains train my eyes *upward*. Lord, I so often fix my eyes on the pebbles at my feet, on the trivialities that trip me and dog my path. Give me Your eyes, Lord. Give me the long view. Thank You for this trail I am on, Lord, the sights along the way, and the vista that awaits at the end. Amen.

Let the rivers clap their hands, let the mountains sing together for joy.
PSALM 98:8 NIV

....

....

....

....

....

....

....

....

....

....

....

....

....

....

....

....

....

Right Motives

God, I admit that sometimes I am guilty of treating my prayers as a wish list to a Santa-God. Or maybe I treat You as though You were a vending machine—if I say the right words in the right order, I'll get what I want. If I'm honest, I know that selfishness and greed may slip into a request here or there. Today I ask that You show me when my prayers are corrupted by selfish desires. Give me pure motives, a pure heart, and a clear conscience.

Ye ask, and receive not, because ye ask amiss,
that ye may consume it upon your lusts.
JAMES 4:3 KJV

....
....
....
....
....
....
....
....
....
....
....
....
....
....
....
....
....

Confidence

As I pray, Lord, I rest in the confidence that You are always listening and that You understand the thoughts behind my prayers, even when I cannot. I am never speaking into empty air! Thank You for the confidence I also experience through the power of Your Holy Spirit that lives inside my heart. With You on my side, I can accomplish much for Your kingdom!

And this is the confidence that we have in him, that,
if we ask any thing according to his will, he heareth us.
1 JOHN 5:14 KJV

....
....
....
....
....
....
....
....
....
....
....
....
....
....
....
....
....
....

The Truth

When I pray to You, God, I pray in Your Son's name. He is the Way, He is the Truth, and He will show me the way to You so that I can live the life that You intend for me. Help me to not be distracted by other false paths that may seem attractive or easier. Make my journey one that invites others to follow me, just as I follow Christ.

Jesus saith unto him, I am the way, the truth, and the life:
no man cometh unto the Father, but by me.
JOHN 14:6 KJV

....
....
....
....
....
....
....
....
....
....
....
....
....
....
....
....
....
....
....

United in Prayer

Thank You, Lord, for others who share my faith in You. Thank You for the privilege of praying with them, for worshipping with them, for working together to build Your kingdom. Thank You that when we pray together, You hear us and that when we gather together, You are there with us. Help us to be the living, breathing, and active body of Christ that we are meant to be.

I say unto you, That if two of you shall agree on earth as touching any thing that they shall ask, it shall be done for them of my Father which is in heaven.
MATTHEW 18:19 KJV

....
....
....
....
....
....
....
....
....
....
....
....
....
....
....
....
....
....

Dry Mouth

Lord, You can use anyone to spread the good news. You can use invalids, the elderly, fishermen, the mentally challenged, paupers, rich men, tax collectors, children, even me. Thank You that You don't require me to know everything or have every answer. You don't require me to be well traveled or well dressed. You don't require a seminary degree. You don't require me to be anything but saved by the blood of Jesus. The only requirement for evangelism is that I believe and speak. Lord, I believe. Now open my mouth.

We also believe and therefore speak.
2 CORINTHIANS 4:13 NKJV

....
....
....
....
....
....
....
....
....
....
....
....
....
....
....
....
....

To a God Who Made Giraffes

Dear Lord, I praise You for laughter. Tonight I laughed until my sides ached, and it was *good*. Now I feel cleansed and emptied of distress and strangely content. Thank You for being a God whose miracles bring laughter: Sarah with the news of her improbable baby, Lazarus raised to life, and the disciples with their ridiculous catch of fish. I can imagine You standing there, Lord, and laughing until the tears came with the people You love. Thank You for giraffes and hedgehogs and zebras and penguins, and how You long to astonish us with joy. Amen.

Then our mouth was filled with laughter
and our tongue with joyful shouting.
PSALM 126:2 NASB

....
....
....
....
....
....
....
....
....
....
....
....
....
....
....
....
....

Well Begun Is Half Done

Dear God, there is something You've asked me to do that I've been putting off for a long time. You haven't forgotten—though *I've* certainly tried to. You keep gently reminding and prodding me to obey. Tonight, as I was walking and pondering this in the darkness between streetlights, I was filled with a cheerful certainty that by the next day, I would have begun. And this wasn't wishful thinking, was it, Lord? It was *faith.* Thank You for believing in what is not yet visible in me and allowing me to do the same. Amen.

Now faith is the substance of things hoped for,
the evidence of things not seen.
HEBREWS 11:1 NKJV

....
....
....
....
....
....
....
....
....
....
....
....
....
....
....
....
....

In All My Ways

God, I claim Your presence in each aspect of my life. Thank You for Your steadfast love and abounding grace. I honor You alone with my successes and acknowledge Your guiding hand on my life. Help me set my eyes only on You. Teach me what it is to trust You with all my heart and to not lean on my own wisdom or understanding. May my heart always seek to bring glory to Your name and may my prayers always reflect this reality.

In all thy ways acknowledge him, and he shall direct thy paths.
PROVERBS 3:6 KJV

....
....
....
....
....
....
....
....
....
....
....
....
....
....
....
....
....
....

The Giver

Lord, I've never been hungry; I've never been naked; I've never been without shelter. You have been a faithful provider of the things You know I need. Thank You for my parents, who provided for me from birth to age twenty-three. And thank You for my husband, who has so faithfully provided for me in the years since then. Thank You, Lord, for providing for me through their generosity and hard work. It's humbling to realize that I've never been completely self-sufficient at any point in my life, yet there is a lesson in that, too. We are paupers by nature: *all* is from You. I praise my open-handed God! Amen.

You open your hand and satisfy the desires of every living thing.
PSALM 145:16 NIV

....
....
....
....
....
....
....
....
....
....
....
....
....
....
....
....
....
....

Willing

I give You, God, everything I have to offer, willingly and gladly. I know that everything I have You have provided and entrusted to me. Give me a whole heart to follow after You and keep Your commandments. Keep forever in my heart Your purposes and thoughts. Show me anything I am holding back. I want You to have it all.

I know also, my God, that thou triest the heart, and hast pleasure in uprightness. As for me, in the uprightness of mine heart I have willingly offered all these things.
1 CHRONICLES 29:17 KJV

....
....
....
....
....
....
....
....
....
....
....
....
....
....
....
....
....

Truthful Heart

Lord, sometimes I lie to myself. Sometimes I try to lie to You. But You know me. You know my thoughts before I think them. Reveal to me Your truth so that my prayers may be true, righteous, and upright. Show me how to live a blameless life.

Lord, who shall abide in thy tabernacle? Who shall dwell in thy holy hill?
He that walketh uprightly, and worketh righteousness,
and speaketh the truth in his heart.
PSALM 15:1–2 KJV

....
....
....
....
....
....
....
....
....
....
....
....
....
....
....
....
....
....

His Work

God, I am amazed that You never tire of listening to me. *I* get tired of listening to me, Lord! The same fears, the same complaints, the same problems, the same confusions—year after year. Yet, even I see progress, and I praise You. I am not who I was, and I know it's all because of You. Thank You for how You continue to work in me: so faithfully, patiently, lovingly. You are the Potter; I am the grateful clay in Your hands. Amen.

"For the eyes of the Lord are on the righteous
and his ears are attentive to their prayer."
1 PETER 3:12 NIV

....
....
....
....
....
....
....
....
....
....
....
....
....
....
....
....
....

One Mind

Unite me in prayer with others, Father God. Let no division come between us as we talk with You. Give me patience in dealing with people who aren't exactly like me and can be trying; remind me that patience will build up Your church. Forgive me for any gossip or malicious words I've spoken against my brothers and sisters and give me a heart that longs for their good. Bring to my mind ways I can show love that will bring more glory to You.

That ye may with one mind and one mouth glorify God,
even the Father of our Lord Jesus Christ.
ROMANS 15:6 KJV

....
....
....
....
....
....
....
....
....
....
....
....
....
....
....
....
....

Believing

I believe in You, Jesus. I believe in Your power and wisdom and love. I believe that Your atoning work on the cross has washed me of all my unrighteousness and that through it, I stand in perfect righteousness before God. Take my life—all my words and deeds—and use them for Your glory. Teach me to trust You, not requiring proof as Thomas did, but believing You at Your Word alone. Thank You that Your Word is truth and brings life to me and to those around me.

Be not faithless, but believing.
JOHN 20:27 KJV

....
....
....
....
....
....
....
....
....
....
....
....
....
....
....
....
....

Joint Heirs with Christ

Thank You, Lord, for adopting me into Your family, for making me Your heir, just as Jesus is. There's nothing I can do to deserve this favor or this acceptance. Your grace is all-sufficient. I now call Jesus my brother, and together we share in Your amazing glory!

For ye have not received the spirit of bondage again to fear; but ye have received the Spirit of adoption, whereby we cry, Abba, Father. The Spirit itself beareth witness with our spirit, that we are the children of God: and if children, then heirs; heirs of God, and joint-heirs with Christ.
ROMANS 8:15–17 KJV

....
....
....
....
....
....
....
....
....
....
....
....
....
....
....
....
....
....

Grace for Everything

Father, I'm thankful for Your *grace* — Your unmerited favor to me through Jesus Christ and that special strength You give Your children in times of need, trial, and temptation. If not for Your grace, I wouldn't even be able to approach You. Thank You for extending favor to me: forgiving my sins and adopting me into Your family. And thank You so much for that extra dose of perseverance that You keep giving to me in tough situations. I'm so thankful Your resource center will never experience a shortage. I praise You today for grace. Amen.

But he gives us more grace.
JAMES 4:6 NIV

....

....

....

....

....

....

....

....

....

....

....

....

....

....

....

....

....

....

....

The Lord Almighty

You, God, can do all things, for You are almighty, all-powerful. Because You are my Father, I know I can trust You to handle each and every aspect of my life. Show me new ways that I can rely on You to work in a mighty way in my life. I trust You with my past, my present, and my future. You are God, and I am not—and I am thankful that's the way it is.

And [I] will be a Father unto you, and ye shall be my sons and daughters, saith the Lord Almighty.
2 CORINTHIANS 6:18 KJV

....
....
....
....
....
....
....
....
....
....
....
....
....
....
....
....
....
....

Arise and Go

So many times, Lord, I feel the urge to drop to my knees and pray. Yet I don't. Embarrassment, busyness, a dirty floor—they can all stop me from heeding Your call. Yet I praise You that You keep calling my name again and again. Please help me to trust You enough to stop what I am doing when I hear Your call. I am on my knees now, my King. I am listening to Your voice.

The word which came to Jeremiah from the LORD, saying: "Arise and go down to the potter's house, and there I will cause you to hear My words."
JEREMIAH 18:1–2 NKJV

....
....
....
....
....
....
....
....
....
....
....
....
....
....
....
....
....
....
....

God of All Comfort

You comfort me, Father, when my heart aches. When everything in my life seems to be going wrong. . .when the world is full of violence and disaster. . .when loss is everywhere I look. . .when hope is dying inside me, Your comfort never fails. Thank You for offering me that constant care in my life. Help me to always extend comfort, care, and compassion to others as well—ultimately leading them to You.

Blessed be God. . .the Father of mercies, and the God of all comfort.
2 Corinthians 1:3 kjv

....
....
....
....
....
....
....
....
....
....
....
....
....
....
....
....
....
....

Living Words

Dear God, Your Word is thousands of years old and tells stories even older. How many books made millennia ago are still useful today? Curious, maybe, or *interesting*, but still practical? Lord, I can't think of even one. We read old poems, histories, and sagas for school assignments or because we want to learn about the past or because they tell good stories, but how many lives have been changed from reading *Beowulf* or *The Canterbury Tales*? Your Word is as true today as when the ink was wet. It is beautiful. It is inspiring. It is rich. It surprises. It sustains. It transforms. I praise the living Word.

O LORD, You are my God. I will exalt You, I will praise Your name, for You have done wonderful things; Your counsels of old are faithfulness and truth.
ISAIAH 25:1 NKJV

....
....
....
....
....
....
....
....
....
....
....
....
....
....
....
....

Spirit-Led

Father, let Your Spirit lead me in each thing. Let me always look to You for guidance and direction. Keep me away from the temptation of following the paths of other "gods." Make Your Spirit alive and active in my heart, so that I might hear Your voice every day, in my every decision, and in my every action. Forgive me when I ignore the movement of Your Spirit. Make Him active in my heart, Lord!

For as many as are led by the Spirit of God, they are the sons of God.
ROMANS 8:14 KJV

....
....
....
....
....
....
....
....
....
....
....
....
....
....
....
....
....
....
....

Peace

Thank You, Father, for the gift of Your peace. Help me to remember that Your peace is the only true and lasting rest for my soul—and to always run to You and no other idol in my life. When troubles come my way, please give me an extra dose of Your peace. And when I see others in turmoil, help me to always be ready with a word and an action that will help them seek out Your peace.

Grace unto you, and peace, from God our Father.
2 THESSALONIANS 1:2 KJV

....
....
....
....
....
....
....
....
....
....
....
....
....
....
....
....
....
....

Alchemy for a Rainy Day

Dear Lord, it's so dark this morning. I know You've already pushed the sun up over the horizon: it is day, though it doesn't feel like it. I don't want to have to pray this morning, Lord. I just want to be where You are. I don't want to be here, in this gray light, with a longer grayness stretching before me, then darkness again. I want to be with You, walking on streets of gold, with the light of Your glory shining on my face. I long for that endless golden day, Lord. But I am here, and You are not far off. Please come to me, Lord, and shine Your love and light on my heart this morning. Amen.

My voice shalt thou hear in the morning, O LORD; in the morning will I direct my prayer unto thee, and will look up.
PSALM 5:3 KJV

....
....
....
....
....
....
....
....
....
....
....
....
....
....
....

What Manner of Love

A good father protects his children; he loves his children unconditionally; he understands and forgives his children; he provides for his family; he is intimately involved in the lives of those he loves. You are more than a good father, God—You are the *perfect* Father. Remind me, Lord, that *this* is the way You love me. Thank You for loving all of me—unconditionally and without reservation.

Behold, what manner of love the Father hath bestowed upon us, that we should be called the sons of God.
1 JOHN 3:1 KJV

....
....
....
....
....
....
....
....
....
....
....
....
....
....
....
....
....
....

A Father's Mercy

Thank You, Lord, that You will never take Your mercy away from me. No matter how many times I let You down, I can always count on You to pick me back up. I cannot understand this gift, but I am thankful for it, Father. Please show me ways to extend mercy to others in my life—especially to those whom the world may deem as "unlovable." Because the truth is, God, I know that most days I, too, am unlovable.

I will be his father, and he shall be my son: and I will not take my mercy away from him.
1 Chronicles 17:13 KJV

....
....
....
....
....
....
....
....
....
....
....
....
....
....
....
....
....

The Living Fossil

Lord, You have preserved Your Word for thousands of years. It is uncorrupted, it is unchanged, it has not been forgotten. Like an animal buried and hammered into rock by time and pressure, it has come down to us, yet it is not fossilized: it lives! You chiseled Your law into rock for Moses, but now Your Word is written in our hearts. And we, too, will live uncorrupted and unforgotten, but, thanks be to You, *changed*. Amen.

You are an epistle of Christ. . .written not with ink but by the Spirit of the living God, not on tablets of stone but on tablets of flesh, that is, of the heart.
2 CORINTHIANS 3:3 NKJV

....
....
....
....
....
....
....
....
....
....
....
....
....
....
....
....
....

Luther, Wesley, Crosby...

Dear God, I don't know where I'd be tonight without the great hymns of the faith that have resounded in my head since I was a girl. Thank You for that legacy of music and poetry and for what You have taught me through meditating on those lines. I praise You for the men and women who penned the lyrics and music that still minister to Christians today. Thank You for the hymns that kept my heart tuned to You, even when I thought I was running far away. Great is thy faithfulness! Amen.

Let the word of Christ dwell in you richly in all wisdom; teaching and admonishing one another in psalms and hymns and spiritual songs, singing with grace in your hearts to the Lord.
COLOSSIANS 3:16 KJV

....

....

....

....

....

....

....

....

....

....

....

....

....

....

....

....

....

Getting to Know You

Dear Lord, thank You for reminding me today to pray for the people who witnessed to me before I was a believer. I was so ignorant of Your ways, Lord, that I didn't even know that was what they were doing! I thought they were just telling me about their lives, that we were getting to know each other, when really they were introducing me to their Savior. I praise You for how real You were to them and for their example of how sharing our faith is more about *conversation* than conversion. Bless those brave evangelists, Lord, and continue to do Your work through them. Amen.

*We loved you so much, we were delighted to share with
you not only the gospel of God but our lives as well.*
1 THESSALONIANS 2:8 NIV

....
....
....
....
....
....
....
....
....
....
....
....
....
....
....
....

Twenty-Four

I thank You for this day, Lord, with its twenty-four precious, exhausting hours. Only twenty-four. That never seems like enough, yet I'm always glad to fall into bed when they're over. Some hours spent in sleep, some in work, some in eating, some in talking, some in staring out the kitchen window at the trees and sky. How many of those hours do I give to You, Lord? Not even *one*, maybe two on Sundays? Thank You for continuing to remind me that relationships require *time*, and I vow to give You more of each day—each day that is already a gift from You. Amen.

This is the day which the LORD hath made; we will rejoice and be glad in it.
PSALM 118:24 KJV

....
....
....
....
....
....
....
....
....
....
....
....
....
....
....
....
....

The Dead Will Live!

Dear Lord, I was feeling so sad this morning. Maybe it was partly the rain and the gray skies, but I was missing certain people so badly. My dad, my grandmothers, my great-aunts, friends. They are all dead, Lord, and that seems so strange and wrong. They are in the ground, out of sight, out of reach. Thank You for comforting me with the assurance that it *is* wrong, that death was not part of Your plan. And that, ultimately, it will be swallowed up in victory. My dad, my grandmothers, they will wake up and shout for joy. Hallelujah!

But your dead will live, LORD; their bodies will rise —
let those who dwell in the dust wake up and shout for joy.
ISAIAH 26:19 NIV

....
....
....
....
....
....
....
....
....
....
....
....
....
....
....

Call to Me

O, Lord of the universe, You know everything; You see everything; You are everywhere; You are every*time* and eternal. Lord, sometimes we think that we are so smart, we people that You *made*. Compared to You, we are babies one minute old, looking up at the light and blinking, unable to comprehend anything. But You want us to grow up, Lord. You long to teach us everything You know. I yield my heart and mind to You. Amen.

"Call to me and I will answer you and tell you
great and unsearchable things you do not know."
JEREMIAH 33:3 NIV

....
....
....
....
....
....
....
....
....
....
....
....
....
....
....
....
....

Make Me Wiser

Dear Father, today I stumbled up against something that calls for Your wisdom. Someone might be in trouble, Lord. But it's a delicate situation, and I might be wrong. I've been wrong before, You know, and stepped out to offer help without Your blessing and just made things worse. I want to be used by You in people's lives, but first I need Your wisdom. I'm no Solomon, Lord, but just like he did, I'm asking for Your wisdom. Thank You that You promise to give it to me freely and generously. And please protect the woman with the bruised cheek. Amen.

If any of you lacks wisdom, let him ask of God, who gives to all liberally and without reproach, and it will be given to him.
JAMES 1:5 NKJV

....

....

....

....

....

....

....

....

....

....

....

....

....

....

....

....

....

Who Knows?

Father, I'm grateful for being Your child in this life. I can't even imagine what that will mean in the life to come! Thank You for the hope You have given to me for now and for an unknown future. Although I don't know all the details of what You have in store, I am thankful I can rest secure, knowing You have it all under control.

Beloved, now are we the sons of God,
and it doth not yet appear what we shall be.
1 JOHN 3:2 KJV

....
....
....
....
....
....
....
....
....
....
....
....
....
....
....
....
....
....
....

Listen to the Music

Dear Father, I'm lifting up a teenager to You tonight who gives You lip service but whose heart doesn't belong to You yet. She knows what to say when Christians are watching, but I know her answers are different when she is in other company. Lord, You are watching her. Remind her of this. Hound her, Lord, until she turns her heart to You. But in this I praise You: she only listens to Christian music. Her soul is yearning for You, whether she knows it or not. Fan that small spark of desire into an eternal *yes*. Amen.

The Spirit and the bride say, "Come." And let the one who hears say,
"Come." And let the one who is thirsty come; let the one
who wishes take the water of life without cost.
REVELATION 22:17 NASB

....
....
....
....
....
....
....
....
....
....
....
....
....
....
....

Worry Lines

Dear Lord, I praise You for how You are changing me. I praise You for how You are teaching me to place a worry in my open hand and lift it up to You: if it stays or if it flies away, it belongs to You. I trust You with my life. Lord, the only worry lines I want are the creases in the pages of my Bible. I praise You that *You* are the overcomer; *You* are my resting place; *You* are my strength and my fortress. I am so relieved to lay my worries before You and let them become prayers. Amen.

Don't fret or worry. Instead of worrying, pray. Let petitions and praises shape your worries into prayers, letting God know your concerns.
PHILIPPIANS 4:6 MSG

....
....
....
....
....
....
....
....
....
....
....
....
....
....
....
....
....
....
....

The Rock

Dear Father, I have a recurring skeptic in my life. He won't give up or give in, and nothing I say seems to make any difference in his opinion of You or Your Word. He's clinging to nothingness like a limpet on a rock, and I can't pull him off. Lord, I am weary of this fight, and I want to give up. But I know I am here because You put me here with this stubborn mollusk (whom You love). Please give me the strength to keep trying, lovingly and gently, to pry him loose from the big lie he is holding on to. *You* are the only Rock. Amen.

For the Word that God speaks is alive and full of power. . .it is sharper than any two-edged sword, penetrating to the dividing line of the breath of life (soul) and [the immortal] spirit.
HEBREWS 4:12 AMPC

....
....
....
....
....
....
....
....
....
....
....
....
....
....
....

Who Are Your Philistines?

I am not a warrior, Lord. I am a weak woman. You know how many push-ups I can do, how many miles I can run, how long I can go without rest. But I have enemies, too. Enemies of anger, self-control, discontent, pride, selfishness, laziness. Strengthen me today for my battles against these foes. You are my high commander, Lord. Strengthen me with Your Spirit so I will be able to resist the enemy of my soul and follow only You. Amen.

"The LORD will cause your enemies who rise against you
to be defeated before your face; they shall come out
against you one way and flee before you seven ways."
DEUTERONOMY 28:7 NKJV

....

....

....

....

....

....

....

....

....

....

....

....

....

....

....

....

The God of Our Salvation

When I start to look to other things for my salvation—money, prestige, people, things—remind me, God, that You are the only One who can save me now and keep me safe forever. Remove the temptations from my life that I am so quick to turn to when I'm stressed and insecure. Make me aware of the pitfalls that surround me. Focus my attention on You and Your kingdom.

Help us, O God of our salvation, for the glory of thy name: and deliver us, and purge away our sins, for thy name's sake.
PSALM 79:9 KJV

....
....
....
....
....
....
....
....
....
....
....
....
....
....
....
....
....

Here Are My Mother and Brothers

Dear Father, sometimes I feel like I'd do better on a desert island. It's hard to live in community. Our rough edges meet the rough edges of others, and the results are scrapes and sparks and *wounds*. Thank You so much for the pictures You present in the Gospels of Jesus living with His disciples. Lord, nothing teaches me more about what pleases You and what is *possible* than studying how You did it, how You lived and loved and ate and traveled, together. Help me think of the people I rub elbows with as *my* disciples, companions, and teachers. Amen.

Pointing to his disciples, he said, "Here are my mother and my brothers. For whoever does the will of my Father in heaven is my brother and sister and mother."
MATTHEW 12:49–50 NIV

....
....
....
....
....
....
....
....
....
....
....
....
....
....
....
....

A Godly Confidence

Dear Lord, there are so many things I want. Sometimes I feel like my prayers are just a long list of wishes, as though You're some sort of celestial genie. But I'm so thankful You are not. You don't give me what I want, just because I want it. I thank You that You give me only what is in line with Your will for me. So, Lord, show me what that is. Reveal Your will, and show me how and for what You want me to pray.

Now this is the confidence that we have in Him,
that if we ask anything according to His will, He hears us.
1 JOHN 5:14 NKJV

....
....
....
....
....
....
....
....
....
....
....
....
....
....
....
....
....

Little Altars All Over

Lord, how easily we forget Your faithfulness. I think *I* would never be like the Israelites, longing for the slave-grown melons and cucumbers of Egypt while following the fire of God through the desert. But my memory is just as short, just as fickle. You knew they needed reminders, so their path was littered with altars and memorials, their calendar marked with feasts and holidays and fasts. *"Don't forget who I Am and what I have done,"* You say. Lord, please show me tangible ways to remember Your faithfulness to me, too. Amen.

Then let us arise and go up to Bethel, and I will make there an altar to God Who answered me in the day of my distress and was with me wherever I went.
GENESIS 35:3 AMPC

....
....
....
....
....
....
....
....
....
....
....
....
....
....
....
....
....

Falling

Dear Father, we started falling in Eden, and we haven't hit bottom yet. Today I said some things I regret. And the things I didn't say (the things only *You* heard) were even worse. I hurt people I care about, and worse, I hurt You, Lord. I am so sorry. Please forgive me. Please redeem my angry, selfish words. I am so glad that You tell us in Your Word to forgive seventy times seven times because I know that is how many times You will forgive me. Thanks be to Jesus, when I fall, I am falling into Your arms. Amen.

Cast your cares on the LORD and he will sustain you;
he will never let the righteous be shaken.
PSALM 55:22 NIV

....
....
....
....
....
....
....
....
....
....
....
....
....
....
....
....
....

Peacemakers

Dear Lord, teach me that if I want the world to see me as Your child, then I need to always work for peace in the world around me. Help me resist the temptation to stir up bitterness or anger among my family, friends, and neighbors. Take away angry, jabbing words that may well up in the heat of the moment. Instead, teach me to be a peacemaker—so that others can't help but acknowledge that You are living and active within me.

Blessed are the peacemakers: for they shall be called the children of God.
MATTHEW 5:9 KJV

....
....
....
....
....
....
....
....
....
....
....
....
....
....
....
....
....
....

The Watcher

Lord, I'm scared. I'm scared of someone I love getting sick. I'm scared of not having enough money. I'm scared of our country falling apart. I'm scared of being abandoned. I'm scared of hurting the ones I love. I'm scared of stepping on snakes. I'm scared of being laughed at. I'm scared that I'll grow old and die before You return. But mostly I'm scared of never knowing You better than I know You right now. Thank You for that fear, Lord, and how it drives me to my knees again and again. Amen.

The Lord will keep you from all harm—he will watch over your life;
the Lord will watch over your coming and going both now and forevermore.
PSALM 121:7–8 NIV

....
....
....
....
....
....
....
....
....
....
....
....
....
....
....
....
....

God's Offspring

The world tells me to be independent, self-sufficient, and to stand on my own two feet. But the truth is that I am intimately connected to the Lord of the universe, and I rely on You for my life, Father. Most days it's a relief that it's not all on me to handle everything. To put it another way, You and I are kinfolk, Lord! I would not exist if it were not for You.

For in him we live, and move, and have our being. . .
for we are also his offspring.
ACTS 17:28 KJV

....
....
....
....
....
....
....
....
....
....
....
....
....
....
....
....
....
....
....

Loving Our Enemies

Heavenly Father, You know I have a hard time loving some of the people in my life. Some of them are downright nasty to me. But Your Word says that You want me to repay evil with good. Remind me that You ask me as Your child to not only love my enemies but to also do them positive, active good, without thought of reward. It's not going to be easy, Lord, but with Your help, I can do it.

But love ye your enemies, and do good, and lend, hoping for nothing again; and your reward shall be great, and ye shall be the children of the Highest.
LUKE 6:35 KJV

....
....
....
....
....
....
....
....
....
....
....
....
....
....
....
....
....
....

Praying Like Breath

Lord, You gave me life, and I praise You. You filled my lungs with air from my very first breath, and I praise You. I praise You because I am fearfully and wonderfully made. Forgive me for not always loving this body You have given me like the amazing creation and great gift that it is. Today, Lord, I want to pray to You like I breathe: in and out, all day long. Fill my mouth with Your praise. Let my lips be always whispering Your name. Let my heart beat to the rhythm of Your perfect will. Amen.

Rejoice always; pray without ceasing.
1 Thessalonians 5:16–17 nasb

....

....

....

....

....

....

....

....

....

....

....

....

....

....

....

....

....

....

The Wedding March

Dear Father, my kids are all still little and know nothing of romantic desire. They are still in love with me and their father. But I know the day is coming, Lord, when they will transfer their affections to someone else, and I lift those yet-unknown *someones* up to You. Bless their future spouses with faith and wisdom and purity as they wait. I pray that You would help me show my children what marriage can be, and that You would hold their hearts, Lord, until You join them with another. Amen.

He who finds a wife finds a good thing, and obtains favor from the LORD.
PROVERBS 18:22 NKJV

....
....
....
....
....
....
....
....
....
....
....
....
....
....
....
....
....
....

If I Can?!

God, You are so amazing! When You first saved me, I suddenly felt like the world had shifted under me, and anything was possible. Even simple, mundane things such as breathing, eating, and looking up at the sky were made new. The knowledge that You did miracles (and might for me, too) made me feel like I was standing on the edge of a new kind of life that was so beautiful and grand I might explode with joy. But it's not just a feeling, Lord. Anything *can* happen. I praise You with open wonder. Amen.

Jesus said, "If? There are no 'ifs' among believers. Anything can happen."
MARK 9:23 MSG

....
....
....
....
....
....
....
....
....
....
....
....
....
....
....
....
....

The Confidence of Firsthand Knowledge

Lord, it all comes down to knowing You. Who I am, where I'm headed, and what You require of me all depend on who You are. I don't ask for supernatural revelation, Lord (though I wouldn't turn it down). I just ask for a dogged determination to know You better, verse by verse. I ask—beg, really—for a continual filling of Your Spirit so that my eyes and heart are wide open to You. Then I can say *amen* with confidence. And I will: Amen!

I've got my eye on the goal, where God is beckoning us onward—to Jesus. I'm off and running, and I'm not turning back.
PHILIPPIANS 3:14 MSG

....
....
....
....
....
....
....
....
....
....
....
....
....
....
....
....
....
....

The Salvation of Everyone!

Dear God, sometimes I get weary waiting for You. I am not patient about waiting for the things I long for with all my heart. But I know You are patient, Lord. You are waiting. You are waiting for *us*. Oh, thank You, that You won't return until everyone has had a chance to hear the Gospel. Thank You that Your incredible patience and love is greater than our persistent sin. Who can I tell, Lord? Who is near me who hasn't yet heard or understood the good news? Even so, come, Lord Jesus. Amen.

For I am not ashamed of the gospel of Christ: for it is the power of God unto salvation to every one that believeth.
ROMANS 1:16 KJV

....
....
....
....
....
....
....
....
....
....
....
....
....
....
....
....

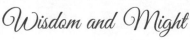

Wisdom and Might

You, Lord, are all-wise. You make the wisdom of the world look like nothing but foolishness. I will never fully grasp the vastness of Your wisdom, but I am thankful to have that strength in my corner. Scripture says that along with being all-wise, You're all-powerful as well. Speak, and the heavens and the earth are at Your beck and call. No matter how powerful we humans think we are, You are the One who holds it all. Today I "hallow Your name" by relying on Your wisdom and might.

Blessed be the name of God for ever and ever: for wisdom and might are his.
DANIEL 2:20 KJV

....
....
....
....
....
....
....
....
....
....
....
....
....
....
....
....
....
....
....

The Cheerleader

Dear Lord, In this verse I can hear You cheering me on. What can I do? *All things!* Who's going to help me? *Christ!* What's He going to do? *Strengthen me!* I praise You for bringing these particular words to me right now. Your Word is so amazing: written thousands of years ago, yet it speaks to us perfectly in our moment of need. What other book is like that? What other god speaks to his people like You do? I know I am going to need this verse today, Lord. Help me to sing it back to You all day long. Amen.

I can do all things through Christ who strengthens me.
PHILIPPIANS 4:13 NKJV

....
....
....
....
....
....
....
....
....
....
....
....
....
....
....
....
....
....

The Construction Site

God, I am a work in progress. Sometimes I feel like there should be a barrier of construction tape and a hedge of warning signs up around all my rough edges. I am not who I want to be yet, Lord, and I know I'm not who *You* want me to be. Yet (and this is such a huge relief and amazement) You love me anyway. Thank You for Your mercy today and always and for the sure promise that You *are* carrying out Your work in me. Give me fertile soil and a yielding heart. Amen.

Being confident of this, that he who began a good work in you
will carry it on to completion until the day of Christ Jesus.
PHILIPPIANS 1:6 NIV

....
....
....
....
....
....
....
....
....
....
....
....
....
....
....
....
....

The God of Hosts

God, my Father, You formed the mountains and the wind, the dark of nighttime and the morning's light, and You lead all the hosts of heaven. You formed my intricate features inside my mother's womb. Let me never take for granted Your limitless creativity. Let me never forget who You truly are.

For, lo, he that formeth the mountains, and createth the wind, and declareth unto man what is his thought, that maketh the morning darkness, and treadeth upon the high places of the earth, The LORD, The God of hosts, is his name.
AMOS 4:13 KJV

....
....
....
....
....
....
....
....
....
....
....
....
....
....
....
....
....
....

Magnifying Glasses

Remind me, Father God, that I am called to be Your magnifying glass. Shine Your light through me to all the world around me. Move me out of the way so that it's all You that others see. My aim is to exalt Your name in everything I do—in thought, word, and deed. Lead me to other people who are like-minded so that we can truly live lives that worship You and only You.

O magnify the LORD with me, and let us exalt his name together.
PSALM 34:3 KJV

....
....
....
....
....
....
....
....
....
....
....
....
....
....
....
....
....
....

Foot Washing

Dear Father, when everything is going well, and people are behaving the way I think they should, I find it easy to love. But when the seas are rougher and the sailors are seasick or muttering mutiny, I am appalled at how quickly I become apathetic or mean-spirited. Forgive me, Lord. I want to love like You do. You washed *Judas's* feet! You gently washed the grimy toes of the man who sold You for thirty pieces of silver. What kind of love is that? I could never do that. But Your Spirit, working through my hands, *could*. I praise You for that and so much more.

"By this everyone will know that you are my disciples, if you love one another."
JOHN 13:35 NIV

....

....

....

....

....

....

....

....

....

....

....

....

....

....

....

....

....

Our Redeemer

You are my Redeemer, Lord—You have saved me from all that separated me from You. When I am not holy, You are. When I am trapped in anxiety and despair, You free me. When I see no hope of escape from my present circumstance, You rescue me. When I feel unworthy and stained beyond all hope of saving, You cover me with grace. I worship Your name, Your presence, Your beauty, and Your strength.

As for our redeemer, the LORD of hosts is his name, the Holy One of Israel.
ISAIAH 47:4 KJV

....
....
....
....
....
....
....
....
....
....
....
....
....
....
....
....
....
....

Baby Blues

Lord, I lift up to You a new mother who is struggling with postpartum depression. With a thirty-six-hour labor, she went from a full-throttle life to a torn body, alien responsibilities, and sleep deprivation. Help her hold on while she heals and adjusts. Surround her with people who will love and support her in practical ways. Be with her husband as he copes with a new baby and a wife who needs him now in ways he never imagined. Bless that little one with health and sleep. Lord, use this time so that they will look back on it and marvel at how You drew them closer to each other and to You. Amen.

He tends his flock like a shepherd: he gathers the lambs in his arms and carries them close to his heart; he gently leads those that have young.
ISAIAH 40:11 NIV

....
....
....
....
....
....
....
....
....
....
....
....
....
....

Don't Touch My Feet

Lord, I'm still thinking about foot washing. I can imagine washing someone else's feet, but the idea of having someone—especially You— wash *my* feet makes me squirm. That is appalling grace, like Your offering Yourself up on the cross for us, an act of love so unbelievable that I sometimes don't know what to do with it. How can I say thank You adequately for that? I don't think I ever can. But I will keep trying: thank You, thank You, thank You. Please take away the embarrassment and pride that so often keep me from running to You for the cleansing I desperately need. Amen.

Jesus answered, "Unless I wash you, you have no part with me."
JOHN 13:8 NIV

....
....
....
....
....
....
....
....
....
....
....
....
....
....
....

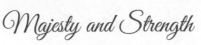

Majesty and Strength

Lord, I admit that the stress of life and the burdens of this world often leave me feeling weak and powerless. But Your name is majesty and strength. Your name is higher, more powerful, and far more excellent than anything this world has to offer me. All I need to do is tap into the power of Your name, and You promise to sustain me. I can do all things through You because You give me strength!

And he shall stand and feed in the strength of the Lord,
in the majesty of the name of the Lord his God.
Micah 5:4 kjv

At Your Nail-Torn Feet

Lord, thank You for the story of Ruth. I love the picture You paint with Boaz, the kinsman-redeemer, and how he rescued a hungry refugee girl and gave her the love, prosperity, and hope she was lacking. And thank You that when You describe Ruth and Boaz, You are also talking about me and my Savior. Since I am Your child, that means Jesus is my kinsman-redeemer, too. I throw myself at Your feet, Jesus. Cover me with Your garment of grace. Live in me. Amen.

I have been crucified with Christ and I no longer live, but Christ lives in me. The life I now live in the body, I live by faith in the Son of God, who loved me and gave himself for me.
GALATIANS 2:20 NIV

....
....
....
....
....
....
....
....
....
....
....
....
....
....
....
....
....

Get Out of Jail Free

Father, the world tells me there's no such thing as a free pass. I need to pay my dues, and then someday I may (if I'm lucky) reap the reward. And of course my actions have consequences—the world is quick to remind me of this as well. But, Father, when I am in trouble—when my soul is in captivity—remind me that all I have to do is call Your name . . .and You will set me free.

Whosoever shall call on the name of the LORD shall be delivered.
JOEL 2:32 KJV

....
....
....
....
....
....
....
....
....
....
....
....
....
....
....
....
....
....
....

Groaning

Dear Lord, my heart and my mind feel empty right now. I don't know how to pray. I don't know what to pray. I just feel like a great weight is sitting on my chest, and I'm afraid the only thing that's going to come out is a horrible noise filled with tears and tiredness. Oh, Father. Thank You that You know I am weak and wordless. Thank You for Your Spirit, my Comforter. Speak for me. Amen.

So too the [Holy] Spirit comes to our aid and bears us up in our weakness; for we do not know what prayer to offer nor how to offer it worthily as we ought, but the Spirit Himself goes to meet our supplication and pleads in our behalf with unspeakable yearnings and groanings too deep for utterance.
ROMANS 8:26 AMPC

....
....
....
....
....
....
....
....
....
....
....
....
....
....
....
....

The Glory of His Name

Lord, fill me with the glory of Your name. May I see the splendor and light of Your character everywhere I turn. When I am burdened, show me evidence of Your love in my daily interactions with others and with Your creation. I want to always be ready with God-filled responses to people who ask about my hope.

Give unto the LORD the glory due unto his name:
bring an offering, and come into his courts.
PSALM 96:8 KJV

....
....
....
....
....
....
....
....
....
....
....
....
....
....
....
....
....
....
....
....

The Hollow

Jesus, when I think about You making Your home in my heart, I imagine a little creature padding a tree hollow with leaves and dry grasses and turning in a tight, furry circle and falling asleep. The tree is strong—an oak, perhaps, or a towering hemlock—and will stand unbowed through the winter storms. I am that furry creature, Lord: a well-beloved, dear thing. And You are the tree. It is not so much that You live in *me*, but that I live in *You*. Thank You for letting me burrow into Your deep, safe, warm heart, Lord, and remain. Amen.

Keep me as the apple of your eye; hide me in the shadow of your wings.
PSALM 17:8 NIV

....
....
....
....
....
....
....
....
....
....
....
....
....
....
....
....
....
....

How's the Service?

Dear Lord, I do a lot of things for a lot of people every day. I serve, then serve some more. But, Lord, I am asking You right now to show me my heart. Is my service pleasing to You? Am I serving under obligation, as one who is a slave to sin? Or am I serving with the voluntary spirit of my freedom in Christ? I long to serve without counting the cost. But it's so easy to pray this sort of prayer, Lord, and then go and *do nothing*. Please show me who and how to serve, then help me do it in Jesus' name. Amen.

"For the LORD searches all hearts and understands all the intent of the thoughts. If you seek Him, He will be found by you."
1 CHRONICLES 28:9 NKJV

....
....
....
....
....
....
....
....
....
....
....
....
....
....
....
....

In Temptation

Dear God, I'm trying to say *no*. Actually I'm trying to say no to this thing You've asked me to stop doing, and I'm trying to say no to You at the same time. I don't want to be double-minded, both asking and doubting: I want Your blessing. So, Lord, help me with my temptation. Other people have struggled with exactly what I am struggling with. It is nothing new, only new to me. But You promise in Your Word that I am strong enough. Help me believe and not doubt. Amen.

No test or temptation that comes your way is beyond the course of what others have had to face. All you need to remember is that God will never let you down; he'll never let you be pushed past your limit; he'll always be there to help you come through it.
1 CORINTHIANS 10:13 MSG

....
....
....
....
....
....
....
....
....
....
....
....
....
....
....

Jesus, in My Heart

Lord, sometimes I think of how the disciples must have felt after they watched You ascend into heaven: bereft, terrified, rootless. You had been everything to them, and suddenly You were gone. *What now?* they must have wondered. But forty days later, You were back. Not just for a visit but to *live* in them forever. Lord, You promise never to leave me or forsake me, and because of the great gift of Your Spirit, I know I am not alone. Thank You that You have made Your home in my heart. Amen.

And I will ask the Father, and He will give you another Comforter (Counselor, Helper, Intercessor, Advocate, Strengthener, and Standby), that He may remain with you forever.
JOHN 14:16 AMPC

....
....
....
....
....
....
....
....
....
....
....
....
....
....
....
....

Singing God's Name

God, fill me with Your song today. Orchestrate within my heart a melody that is truly a joyful noise, one that will bring gladness to Your heart. Give me words of praise to You and words of encouragement for others. Fill my song with Your peace and Your beauty. Help me to live out that song every moment, regardless of my circumstances. May I hallow Your name with singing.

I will praise the name of God with a song,
and will magnify him with thanksgiving.
PSALM 69:30 KJV

....
....
....
....
....
....
....
....
....
....
....
....
....
....
....
....
....
....

In Quietness

Lord, sometimes it feels like I never sit down. There are always so many things to do: people to manage, dishes to wash, bills to pay, groceries to buy, toilets to fix, e-mails to answer. The noise and busyness of my life seem unending. But I know You call me to come away, just as Jesus did, and come to You in quietness and rest. Not just because You desire it, but because that quietness and rest in Your presence is the source of my strength. Thank You for longing to protect my heart in this crazy, merry-go-round world. Amen.

For thus saith the Lord GOD, the Holy One of Israel; in returning and rest shall ye be saved; in quietness and in confidence shall be your strength.
ISAIAH 30:15 KJV

....
....
....
....
....
....
....
....
....
....
....
....
....
....
....
....
....

So Be It

Dearest Lord, I know what I want, but I can't see the future. I know what I think would be best for me and the people around me, but I don't have Your eyes. So I pray, but I hold my prayers lightly. Are they Your will? Am I praying rightly? Show me, Lord. When I pray *Amen*, I think what I really mean is *Your will be done*. And it's a conundrum: I know Your will *will* be done, yet You ask me to pray also. Why, Lord? I long to obey with knowledge, but for now I will simply obey. And wait on You. Amen.

The effective, fervent prayer of a righteous man avails much.
JAMES 5:16 NKJV

A God of Justice

If I hallow Your name, God, then I need to remember just who You really are: a God of justice. Remind me that You have called me to show the same justice in everything I do. Thank You for being the perfect balance of justice and mercy, of fairness and love. Try as I might, I cannot strike that balance in my life without Your help. Teach me to love justice and strive for justice every day.

For I the LORD love judgment, I hate robbery.
ISAIAH 61:8 KJV

....
....
....
....
....
....
....
....
....
....
....
....
....
....
....
....
....
....
....

Strength in Joy

So often, Lord, I walk around with a glum face, as if being a child of the only living God weren't something to cheer about every moment of every day. I complain about how much work I have to do, how little I am appreciated, how relentlessly hard life seems sometimes. But You tell me in this verse to do these things: eat something yummy (thanks, Lord!), drink, share with others. Since Jesus came to earth, every day is a celebration. And Your festival-joy is the strength I need to keep on. Amen.

Nehemiah said, "Go and enjoy choice food and sweet drinks, and send some to those who have nothing prepared. This day is holy to our Lord. Do not grieve, for the joy of the LORD is your strength."
NEHEMIAH 8:10 NIV

The Amen Incarnate

Dear Father, so many portraits paint Jesus as a soft, almost wilting, white man. But I bet You weren't: I bet You were dark and as hard as nails. I bet Your feet were cut and Your hands were scarred, even before the cross. Yet You are also the image of the invisible God. You are the Amen, the *so be it*. There is an equation here, the solution of which is just beyond my grasp. Jesus equals the image of God equals Amen equals *so be it*. I am so glad You are not easy to figure out. I am so thankful that You offer mystery and puzzles and food for thought that will satisfy my soul for eternity. Amen.

> *"These are the words of the Amen, the faithful*
> *and true witness, the ruler of God's creation."*
> REVELATION 3:14 NIV

....
....
....
....
....
....
....
....
....
....
....
....
....
....
....

Called by His Name

Oh God, not only have You adopted me as Your child, but now You say I also have Your name as my own. You pursued me, You purchased me, You accepted me, You love me. Although I don't deserve the honor of being called Yours, I am so happy to accept the gift. Help me strive to be worthy of it.

Thy words were found, and I did eat them; and thy word was unto me the joy and rejoicing of mine heart: for I am called by thy name, O LORD God of hosts.
JEREMIAH 15:16 KJV

....
....
....
....
....
....
....
....
....
....
....
....
....
....
....
....
....
....

Face to Grace

Father, my friend who loves You is dying. Her body is a minefield of cancer; the doctor says she has just weeks to live. Just a few weeks until she sees You face-to-face! But I praise You, Lord, in the midst of my tears because the power of Christ is so visibly resting on her right now, as she stands with her face touching the veil, seeing shadows of the next life. Only You can do this: give a woman, wasting away and saying good-bye to her young family, a joy and strength that evangelizes *others*. Even if You don't heal her, she is giving You all the glory. And I am seeing Your wonders. Amen.

And He said to me, "My grace is sufficient for you, for My strength is made perfect in weakness." Therefore most gladly I will rather boast in my infirmities, that the power of Christ may rest upon me.
2 CORINTHIANS 12:9 NKJV

....

....

....

....

....

....

....

....

....

....

....

....

....

....

A Mustard Seed

Lord, in order for Your kingdom to grow and expand, please plant a seed of faith in my heart. Make my heart a fertile place for that faith to grow so that my work in Your kingdom will be fruitful. Embolden Your Spirit in me so that I might contribute greatly to Your plans—not for my glory but for Yours alone, Father.

The kingdom of God. . .is like a grain of mustard seed, which, when it is sown in the earth, is less than all the seeds that be in the earth.
MARK 4:30–31 KJV